CATHOLIC MISSIONS

IN

SOUTHERN INDIA

TO 1865

CATHOLIC MISSIONS

IN

SOUTHERN INDIA

TO 1865

REV. W. STRICKLAND, S. J.

AND

T. W. M. MARSHALL, ESQ.

Published by

GYAN

Gyan Publishing House
5, Ansari Road
Daryaganj, New Delhi-110002
Phone: 011-47034999, 9811692060
E-mail: books@gyanbooks.com

Distribution Network
gyanbooks.com
India, USA, Canada, UK, Australia, France

ISBN: 978-81-212-9396-9 (PB)
First Published, 1865

2nd Impression 2023

Printed at: Gyan Press, Delhi.

CATHOLIC MISSIONS IN SOUTHERN INDIA TO 1865

AUTHORS: W. STRICKLAND, T. W. M. MARSHALL

CATHOLIC MISSIONS

IN

SOUTHERN INDIA

TO 1865.

BY

REV. W. STRICKLAND, S.J.

TWELVE YEARS MILITARY CHAPLAIN IN INDIA;

AND

T. W. M. MARSHALL, Esq.

AUTHOR OF "CHRISTIAN MISSIONS."

LONDON:

LONGMANS, GREEN, AND CO.

MDCCCLXV.

CONTENTS.

Catholic Missions in Southern India

TO 1865.

CHAPTER I.

THE ENGLISH IN INDIA.

In looking at the Map of the World, there is something astonishing in the consideration that the small spots called the British Islands should contain a people whose influence is felt all over the universe, and whose empire and possessions extend into every climate and into every part of the known world. By far the most valuable of these possessions, both for wealth and population, is the peninsula of Hindostan, containing at least 150,000,000 inhabitants in its vast plains, forests, and mountains. This immense country is peopled by a number of different races and nations, as distinct in personal appearance and language as the various nations of Europe; yet throughout there is a great similarity in manners and customs induced by the influence of the Brahminical religion, which prevails more or less over the whole continent of Hindostan.

The subdivision of the nation into castes, though under different names, prevails every where, and is every where materially the same. The caste of an individual is determined by his birth, and by birth alone; and it is this system of caste which is, as it were, the keystone of Hindoo social life. It has enabled the Hindoos to preserve their nationality, in spite of repeated conquest, and has hindered their being absorbed by their conquerors. Although centuries have elapsed since the Mahommedan conquest, and the Mussulmans have been settled in large numbers over the face of the country, yet they remain quite a distinct and separate people. Though they have domineered and tyrannised over the Hindoos, though they have robbed and plundered them, still the follower of Brahma has kept aloof from the despised Moslem, and no relationship or intercourse of family life has ever existed between the two races. The assertion may appear strange, yet indisputably this division of the people into different castes has contributed immensely to the preservation of public morality, and the conservation of the patriarchal customs which still exist in the country. Those who would allow no fear of God or man to check them in their evil courses, tremble before their caste, and dread that sentence of exclusion which would at once deprive them of the friendship and intercourse of their nearest kindred, and send them as vagrants through the land. In vain the Mahommedan power strove to crush this system—the English were too politic to attempt to meddle with it. No doubt caste has its disadvantages, for when pushed too far it engenders egotism, it destroys true patriotism, and hinders the development of talent. At the same time, it is a salutary check to ambition, an insurmountable barrier to communism and all its attendant evils, and gives a powerful support to those social distinctions which constitute society.* Those who have studied

* In many nations, social distinctions have been determined by military service. Amongst the Chinese, learning is the only introduction to rank and position; amongst the North-American Indians, it was the number of scalps taken in battle; but amongst the Hindoos only has birth alone been at all times sufficient to secure the social position.

the Hindoo in his own country will agree with the remark made by a distinguished English magistrate in India, that without the institution of caste, the Hindoos would long ago have been sunk down to the lowest degree of barbarism, and have literally devoured one another. It would therefore be a mistake for Christianity to attempt to destroy what is good in the customs of caste; the good should rather be developed and improved, whilst so much of these customs only should be rejected as is really inconsistent with the holiness and charity of the Gospel.

The study of this question of caste will throw a great light on many periods of Hindoo history, which it would otherwise be difficult to understand. As, for instance, their early civilisation, at a time when Europe was entirely buried in barbarism, may be explained by the gradual development of knowledge in a family, the fathers teaching their children all they knew, and the children, in their turn, having no idea, or even wish, beyond those things which belonged to their caste and family. This may, probably, have been fatal to the development of great genius, but it certainly contributed to domestic peace and prosperity, whilst at the same time it admitted an amount of development, both in learning and handicraft, which is the more admired the more it is known. The wisest sages of antiquity drew their knowledge from India; and the architectural and mechanical skill of the Hindoos must have been great to raise the buildings which exist, constructed of enormous stones, and to cast the cannon which, only a few years ago, were beyond the skill of our best foundries in Europe. On the other hand, the existence of caste, inasmuch as it prevents national unity, has certainly made the Hindoo an easy prey to the conqueror, invited to invasion by the richness of the country.

From the very earliest times down to the present day, the history of India consists of a succession of conquests: the conquerors have overrun the country, plundered its inhabitants, dwelt for a time dominant amongst them, and then have been swept away, each in their turn, by some subsequent invasion; the Hindoo people, forming all along the great mass of the population, remaining as a body entirely distinct from their successive conquerors. Since the early, and not quite fabulous, expeditions of Bacchus and Hercules down to the present English occupation, there is thus a great similarity in the various chapters of Indian history. Now, as in former times, the races remain separate; and the high-caste Hindoos, whilst submitting to the conqueror, despise him, and await the time when, as has so often happened before, they shall see their present masters told to "move on," and make place for others.

How has the English power been formed in India?—how have their small mercantile stations developed into the immense empire of 150,000,000 who now own the rule of Great Britain and submit to her power,—a power which she has wonderfully shown in upholding her sway in the midst of the most sudden and violent storm of well-organised revolt which history makes mention of? There is a passage in Scripture, in the Book of Macchabees, which, speaking of the Roman power of that time, gives so correct a description of the ways and means by which Great Britain has acquired her Indian territories, that it is worth recording: "Possederunt omnem terram consilio suo et patientiâ." And it is by wisdom in council, and by patiently watching their opportunity, that the English have obtained and kept their hold upon India: wisdom, which certainly has often degenerated into Machiavellism, but has never neglected a single opportunity of aggrandisement;

patience, which has always known how to "bide its time," and to avoid precipitation, which has so often ruined the most brilliant prospects,—waiting for the right moment to strike, and then giving full play to their national energy by striking home at once. It is about 200 years since the English first landed in India, with the intention of holding a mercantile footing in the country, but without the least dream then of realising the empire they now possess. From 1650 to 1750 the English comptoirs or factories gradually developed into citadels and powerful forts; being thus consolidated, from 1750 to 1800 England mixed herself up on every possible occasion with the quarrels of the native princes, always keeping her given word for the time being, but changing sides as interest dictated, so as to weaken each party in succession; at the same time selling her help, where it was afforded, as dearly as possible,—an accession of territory being always a part of the bargain. Edmund Burke declares that she never made an Indian treaty which, at least in spirit, she did not break. England was thus able, as it were, by means of the Indians themselves, to conquer India; for during many of her wars the number of European soldiers, though a necessary element of success, was usually very small. Nothing is more remarkable in the diplomatic history of British India than the skill with which the English Government in the country was always able, even in their utmost need, either by promises or threats, to persuade one or other of the numerous parties in the country to espouse their cause. Being always eventually successful, in spite of some partial reverses, so she was always most careful to keep for a season her promises and fulfil her engagements.

When the might of Hyder Ali and the power of Tippoo Saib were arrayed against them, the English were able to persuade the Nizam and the King of Travancore to espouse their quarrel; and in return, up to the present day, the descendants of these princes enjoy their kingdoms in nominal independence, whilst the territories of Tippoo and Hyder have long since been absorbed into the British empire, or in part bestowed as rewards on the ancient dynasty and others who stood by the English in their day of trial. During this time of Indo-British history there were many remarkable men —Lord Clive, the real founder of the present gigantic power of England in India; also Sir Arthur Wellesley, afterwards the Duke of Wellington—who, by their skill both in council and in the field, contributed to consolidate those schemes of aggrandisement which the successes of Clive first made tangible, or even possible. It would be as impossible to defend all that was done then, and the way in which some of the Indian princes were treated, as it would be to defend many other political histories of the growth of nations. One thing may be, however, urged in palliation,—which is, that there has been more idea of right, more safety to property, and more effort to dispense real justice in India, since she came under British power, than in the whole of her previous history.

There is an important question, however, to which a few words are due—Has India, as a nation, been a gainer or a loser by the English occupation? There is little doubt that the knowledge of the arts and sciences which existed formerly in the country has very much diminished; some few may possess a more varied learning, and a smattering of European knowledge; but education has certainly not gained on the whole. Commerce also has suffered immensely; the country becomes every year more and more impoverished,* and native manufac-

* The *Times* correspondent during the Mutiny said that in India each day the poor were poorer and the rich were richer.

tures, which from time immemorial astonished the world for their skill, have died out, and been supplemented by the large importation of British manufactures. The looms of India, for instance, formerly worked with such wonderful dexterity, considering their very simple construction, are now nearly all idle. The cotton grown in India can be sent in its raw state to Europe, and there manufactured by the aid of machinery, and re-imported, after all the expense of double transport and labour, at a rate so low as to undersell the native weaver. The native cloth, it is true, is far more lasting; but the English calicoes are cheaper, and supply the present want at a smaller price. The same might be said of a number of other manufactures. How, then, has the country gained? In this,—that the people enjoy more peace and tranquillity; that law is administered with far greater justice; that wars cannot go on at the will and caprice of each petty prince, as in former times. The Indian who possesses a field can hope to sow and reap his crops in peace; the man who builds a house can hope to dwell in it; and the merchant who is known to have made a successful speculation can safely possess his gold, without being imprisoned and tortured till he discloses the place where his hoards are concealed. The Indian has, through his whole history, been always a prey to those who were strongest and boldest amongst themselves, or to the conquerors who successively overran their country. Robbery and plunder were an everyday occurrence; and society could never have held together, but for the strange power of passive resistance which the internal organisation, and consequently strong cohesiveness, of caste bestowed on the different bodies, which thus constituted at all times, and with very little change, the mass of the race—for nation it can scarcely be called, nationality, as felt and fostered in Europe, being almost unknown amongst them. The caste customs established by the great Hindoo legislator Manou, all interwoven with and supported by their ideas of religion, have remained almost unchanged from their first institution. On the other hand, the heavy taxes levied on the people by the English Government, amounting often to fifty per cent on the produce of the soil, are too burdensome for the country to bear, and are too high a price to pay for the safety in which they may enjoy what remains to them; yet, on the whole, the amount of order and law which the dominant power and skilful police of the English preserve in the country is so highly appreciated by the people, that, unless they were worked up and excited by emissaries of evil, they would have neither wish nor desire to shake off the British yoke. This was almost unmistakably shown in the late outbreak, which was much more a military rebellion than a popular movement. If it had been heartily supported by the people, it is doubtful if all the power and courage of Great Britain could have regained possession of the country in the very short time in which it was effected.

On the other hand, the advantages which England draws from India are immense; for, granting that the revenues of India scarcely suffice for the expenses of her government,—which is very nearly correct, although the various imports reach the enormous sum of seventy millions sterling,—still the very large field open to her commerce causes incalculable wealth to flow back upon the mother-country of the English who rule and trade in India. Besides this, it is no small advantage to have so fine a field for the expenditure of energy and ambition abroad; for this keeps things quiet at home; and the life, talent, and capital used up and employed in her vast colonies has enabled England to ride peaceably through those great changes in government which have taken place in all countries of late years, and have caused wars and rebellions in the other nations of Europe. In England, every ambitious spirit could find a field for exertion, and every strong hand could earn an honest living—and this, in a great measure, because, by the gradual decay of Indian manufacture, it was so brought about that the 25,000,000 at home had to furnish the 150,000,000 in India with almost every thing they needed beyond their daily food. In addition to this must be considered the large number of people, highly salaried and pensioned for their services to the Government in India, returning home after twenty or twenty-five years' service with a comfortable independence. Taking all these things into account, it shows how immense an advantage, and what a great source of wealth, India has been to England.

From the few preceding pages some slight idea may be formed of the social and political effect of the presence of the English in India. But what most immediately concerns the present purpose is to inquire, briefly, What is the position of the Catholic Church and her clergy in their efforts to preach the faith of Jesus Christ, and preserve their converts amongst the Hindoos thus governed by British rule? It will suffice at present to answer this query in general terms, for it is a constantly recurring subject, and has so many different bearings, that it will reappear more or less directly in several of the chapters of this book.

It has been often imputed to the English, and with much truth, that during the earlier part of their domination in India they so entirely neglected all exteriors of religion, as to be looked upon by the natives as a race without any religion whatever. During this period also they professedly and avowedly abstained from all effort to spread the holy and civilising influence of Christianity amongst their Hindoo subjects, insomuch that the missionaries of the various Protestant societies were strictly forbidden to settle in the country. On various occasions, when some had eluded the vigilance of the Government, and penetrated into the interior, they were most unceremoniously seized, transported to the nearest coast, and put on board ship. Nor was this all; for it is a fact of public history, that until the year 1800 the Government openly and actively supported Paganism as one of the institutions of the country, giving large sums out of the public taxes for carrying out the heathen sacrifices with splendour, because such had previously been the custom of the native princes whom they had supplanted. Up to this time, except where human life was positively concerned, no check whatever was put upon the revolting ceremonies of Hindoo worship, but rather even they were often sanctioned by the presence of the English officials, both civil and military. During the forty succeeding years all open concurrence and participation nearly ceased—though the administration of the funds of the Hindoo temples was still under the supervision of the Government, which also drew a considerable revenue from this source. This official supervision had a conservative effect on Hindooism, inasmuch as it hindered the funds from diminishing either by peculation or extravagance, and provided for all due repairs of the temples and other places connected with them.

Since 1840 the Government ostensibly holds aloof from all interference in religious affairs or properties, and the result has been a great diminution in the available funds, and consequently in the splendour of the Pagan ceremonial. All Hindoo prejudices and customs are still respected with the utmost scruple, and all lands dedicated to the support of the temples are exempt from taxation—no inconsiderable privilege, when their extent is taken into account. If England, during her long sway in India, had quietly discountenanced all acts of idolatry, and officially ignored its existence, except where the civil law required it, she might have done much, without the semblance of persecution or oppression, to prepare the Hindoo for the profession of Christianity, and introduce him to the civilisation inseparable from it. This passive policy is now generally being adopted, and has already produced its fruits.

The probable ultimate result of this passive abstention from all support of heathenism on the part of Government will be its rapid decadence. On the other hand, the same system of indifference observed towards Christianity is producing exactly opposite results.

The position of the Catholic Church at present in India is one of the utmost liberty: she is entirely unaided and unsupported by the Government, but there are now no exceptional restrictions, no penal laws. By the laws of the country now existing, both life and property are secure; so that those who, from a spirit of hostility to the Catholic religion, would wish to be aggressive, can never venture on open acts of persecution either against the missioners or their flocks. This is an immense advantage, and cannot be too highly appreciated. The Catholic missioner, from whatever country he may come to devote his life to the conversion and instruction of the Hindoos, appreciates to the full this great blessing, soon feels cordially loyal to the Government which secures it to him, and inspires this loyalty to his flock.

At the time that the English rule became dominant in India, the Catholic Church was at its lowest ebb. By the suppression of the Society of Jesus in Europe, and the reigning spirit of infidelity, the supply of European missioners was nearly cut off; the Christians were poor, and their priests for the most part without zeal. The very existence of Catholicity seemed almost ignored by Government—it was no advantage to be a Christian; nearly all employments were given in preference to Hindoos and Mussulmans, or Protestant converts. Yet this very obscurity was a protection and a source of liberty. As soon as a fresh vigour was infused into the Catholic body by the renewed labours of zealous European priests, it began to consolidate and develop itself. At the time of the Mutiny there was a moment of alarm lest, by the success of the insurgents, the old times of Pagan domination and Christian suffering might be renewed; and earnest prayers were raised to God from every Catholic home and church in India to avert the scourge. Government, too, in its moment of alarm, remembered its Catholic subjects, and acknowledged their existence by sending *officiously* to inquire of the missioners how their congregations were disposed, and how many men might be available in an emergency. The answer so far exceeded their expectations, that since then the Catholic body in Southern India has enjoyed a little more consideration and respect. They were told that 30,000 able-bodied men were available, who knew the nature and obligation of an oath. At their first return to India, the European Fathers found themselves treated with very scant courtesy by the officials, both civil and military, for the new-comers were priests and foreigners; but as they became better known, they were more appreciated and esteemed; their position is now at least one of acknowledged respectability, and their great influence over their rapidly increasing congregations gives them a position which, joined to their blameless and laborious lives, commands the respect, not only of the Europeans, but also of the Hindoos, amongst whom they dwell.

CHAPTER II.

IDOLATRY IN INDIA AND IN THE MADURA MISSION.

THE Vicariate-Apostolic of Madura is situated in the southernmost part of the peninsula of British India, and contains part of the Southern Carnatic, the provinces of Tanjore, the small but nominally independent territory of the Tondimau, Marava, Madura, and the country down to Cape Comorin. It is bounded on the north by a branch of the river Cauvery, which falls into the sea a little north of Negapatam; on the west by the Coorg chain of hills; on the south and east by the sea. Thus the district extends from about 7° 57′ to 11° 50′ north latitude, and in the widest part is nearly three degrees of longitude. The climate is very relaxing, as the heat is almost continual, even in the months equivalent to our winter; but it is usually dry, except in the periodical rainy seasons. The months of March and April, when the sun is going northward, are so intolerably hot, that every thing that is touched, even in-doors, feels hotter than the hand, and exertion of mind or body is most difficult, except very early in the morning or after sunset. The heat often exceeds 100° Fahr. by day in-doors, and does not fall below 72° in the night; yet this is the healthiest season of the year. In January and February the cholera is very common, arising apparently from the frequent chills, which, though never amounting to cold, are most trying to constitutions enervated by the constant heats. The population may be rated at nearly four millions, partly Hindoos and partly Mussulmans; of the former, about 150,000 are Christians, but the latter uniformly refuse to listen to instruction. The following anecdote will give some idea of their prejudice against Christianity. "A native Christian priest occasionally visited the College at Negapatam; like our European missionaries in India, he wore his beard, which his caste among the Hindoos do not, so that at a short distance he looked more like a Mussulman than a Hindoo. One day he came towards the place where a Mahommedan teacher was giving lessons in Telingoo to some pupils of the College; as he came in sight, the teacher eagerly asked who he was. 'One of our priests,' was the answer. 'But what was he before? was he ever a Mussulman?' asked the *moonshee* with eagerness. 'No, a Hindoo.' 'Oh! well, I am glad. If he had ever been a Mussulman, I would have stabbed him this instant, though I know I should have been hanged for it.'"

A slight sketch of the creed of the Hindoos, by far the most numerous inhabitants of this large district, may be thought interesting, and indeed will be most appropriate as a preface to our account of the introduction and present state and prospects of Christianity in the Vicariate of Madura.

The more learned and sensible among the Hindoos believe in one only God, called by some Chivem, but more commonly Vishnou. They look on him as almighty, and as the source of all life; as the origin of time, the creator of all, the preserver of all, and at last to be the destroyer of all. They even call him the God of gods, the only Lord. He is immense, and, like the light, is present every where; he is eternal, and born of none; he is all things, and will exist in all times; he is infinitely happy, and free from grief and care; truth itself; the source of all justice; the ruler and disposer of all; infinitely wise; without form, without figure, without nature, or name, or caste, or parentage; pure to the exclusion of passion or inclination. He knows himself, and is incomprehensible to all but himself; so that the other deities, who are but his creatures, do not even comprehend his essence. To him the sun and moon owe their light; and his threefold power of Creator, Preserver, and Destroyer are represented in the triple figure called Trimourti. The numberless gods worshiped by the populace are but imagined for minds too rude and weak to do without material and palpable objects of adoration. All this is distinctly contained in their sacred books; and were it practically held, one could scarcely wish a better foundation for Christianity; but not only are the mass of the people buried in perhaps the grossest idolatry recorded in the annals of the human race, but even the very Brahmins, who profess to believe all they find in these books, draw from them ideas strangely similar to that Pantheism now so rapidly spreading in Germany, and which many look upon as the new form of attack planned by the enemy of man against Christian Europe. "All," say the Brahmins, "is Brahm" (another name of the Supreme Being described above); "he is the soul of the world, and of each being in particular; this universe is *Brahm*, it springs from him, subsists in him, and will return to him. He is the self-existent Being, the form of endless worlds, which are all one with him, as they exist through his will, which is revealed alike in the creation, in the preservation, and in the destruction of things, in the movements and in the forms of time and space." It is not difficult to see how inevitably this doctrine must, in uncultivated minds, lead to the grossest idolatry, and such we find to be the fact; for the Hindoos in general have lost all idea of the Unity of God, and have multiplied divinities according to every wild caprice of imagination or passion;

some of them being such as decency will not allow the mind to rest on for an instant. Those that can be described may be briefly detailed as follows:

It has been stated that the *Trimourti, or triple idol*, is originally but the representation of the threefold action of the one supreme God, symbolised in the sacred word *Om*, so holy that few will pronounce it, though it is held as the subject of silent meditation; but it usually bears three names: Brahma, the Creator; Vishnou, the Preserver; and Siva or Chivem, the Destroyer; represented as a figure with three heads, and usually three bodies more or less separated. Most Hindoos adore only one of these powers, but some worship the threefold power.

Brahma, the invisible head of the Brahmins, is an emanation of the supreme, self-existent Brahma above described, and is the priest and lawgiver. He is said to have married Sarassavadi, the goddess of science and of harmony, and is represented with four heads and four arms; in one hand he holds a circle, representing immortality; and in another, fire, the emblem of strength; with a third he writes in a book which he holds in the fourth, to designate legislative power. Some Hindoos think that these represent the four Vedams, or sacred books, which he is said to have written with his own hands on leaves of gold. He has neither temples nor worship nor disciples, having by an impudent lie, to be related hereafter, drawn on himself the anger of Siva, who deprived him of the homage of mortals; but his repentance obtained for him the worship of the Brahmins, who pray to him every morning.

Vishnou is more celebrated; he is represented with four arms, riding on the bird Garouda; his wives are Latchimi, the goddess of riches, and Boumidevi, the goddess of earth. The former bore him Monmadi, who is the Cupid of the Greek mythology, and who is armed with a sugar-cane bow and arrows tipped with flowers, and is mounted on a parrot. He and his wife Radi have no separate temples, but their figures are carved in those of Vishnou.

The sacred books record no fewer than twenty-one incarnations or *avatars* of Vishnou, but nine of these are specially noted; they are too wild and foolish to be worth narrating at length in this place. In the first he became a fish; in the second, a tortoise; in the third, a wild boar; in the fourth, a monster, half-man, half-lion; in the fifth, a Brahmin dwarf, to humble the pride of the giant Bely; in the sixth, a man, to put down the giant Ravanen, King of Ceylon, who made himself be worshiped as a god; in the seventh, a man again, to live in solitude and penance, silently destroying the wicked whom he met with; in the eighth, once more a man, to teach mortals the practice of virtue and detachment from the world; in the ninth, a black shepherd, to exterminate wicked and cruel kings. The tenth avatar is expected impatiently, as the end of the dominion of sin, and the beginning of a new age, in which virtue and happiness will reign alone on earth. Ridiculous as are these transformations, their details would be far more so; yet one finds in them many points of resemblance with the history of Christianity, so striking as to leave no doubt of their being borrowed in part from the religion of Christ or the prophecies of the Old Testament.

Vishnou is the second person of their Trinity, taking flesh to free the world from evil, which had spread so widely as to touch him with pity. He says in one place, "Though by nature not subject to be born or to die,—though I rule all creation,—I yet command my own nature, and make myself visible by my own power; and as often as virtue becomes weak in the world, and vice and injustice rise up, so often I am seen. Thus I appear from age to age to save the just, to destroy the wicked, and to reëstablish tottering virtue." He came on earth by a sacrifice of which he alone was capable, to save it from certain destruction; he subjected himself to all the weaknesses and miseries of humanity, and to a cruel death, to destroy evil, and to make virtue reign; he became a shepherd, a warrior, and a prophet, to leave a pattern to mankind; yet he is all the time the God of all, the representative of the invisible Being by whom he was sent, and powerful, just, good, and merciful like him; compassionate even to his enemies, and requiring from his followers faith and love, and a true and spiritual worship, a desire of being united to him, self-denial, and a contempt of the world; he alone can make people holy, and give eternal happiness. Here again we have ideas which would make the introduction of Christianity easy, were they really current among the people; but unfortunately they are known only to the more learned among them, and even with them have little influence on their practice; they are therefore no check to the grossest idolatry, and all its consequences of systematised sensuality. To continue our sketch of their better known fables: Brahma and Vishnou were struggling for preëminence, and the universe shook with the combat, when the supreme God appeared in the form of an endless column of fire, and, being terrified, they paused. He promised superiority to whichever should first find the extremity of this column, and Vishnou, in the form of a wild boar, spent a thousand years in digging, but in vain. Brahma meanwhile, in the form of a swan, soared upwards for one hundred thousand years, but without success; tired, he went to Vishnou, and told him he had reached the summit of the column, showing, as proof, a flower, which spoke, and confirmed his falsehood; but the column opened, the eight elephants who support the earth spouted blood, the clouds were burned, and the supreme God appeared, laughing derisively, and cursing Brahma, who cast himself at Siva's feet, and received pardon so far as to be worshiped by the Brahmins. Had we space, we might multiply such tales almost infinitely; but we have said enough to excite the gratitude of those to whom truth has been revealed, and to make them pity the millions who are buried in such gross darkness. A petrified shell, called Salagranan, is often worshiped as an idol of Vishnou, because it sometimes has nine different shades of colour, which are considered emblems of these nine avatars. It is carried on a white linen cloth, with the greatest respect, bathed with many ceremonies, and the water is drunk as a means of purification.

Siva, the third god of the Trimourti, has two opposite aspects: under the names of Bhava, Baghis, Bhogovan, &c., he is the father and benefactor of all; his forehead is adorned with a crescent, he rides on the bull Nandi, and holds in his hands the lotus and the good serpent; but under the names of Cala, Hara, Ougra, &c., he seems to change his nature; he is the god of destruction, the conqueror of death and of demons, fearful of aspect, with long, sharp teeth, flames for hair, and human skulls for a necklace; while his girdle, and the bracelets of his many arms, are fierce serpents. He delights in blood and tears and in the most cruel vengeance, and he rides a tiger. The Hindoos of his sect look on him as the only god, and give him a wife named Parvati, who resembles the Phrygian Cybele: she is often worshiped together with him, but sometimes has separate temples.

Their son Pollear presides over marriages; he is represented under the most monstrous forms, and is so venerated that his image appears in every temple, under trees, by the roadsides; and our missionaries have sometimes difficulty in dissuading Christian women from wearing it among their ornaments. But we cannot pursue to their full extent the degrading idolatries of these poor people; their divinities have been said to amount to 33,000,000, and many animals are among the number, especially the monkey, for whom the worshipers of Vishnou have a peculiar regard,—so much so, that they consider it a most meritorious act to give him food, and they salam* to him every morning when they first meet him. The Garouda, or Malabar eagle, is also adored by Vishnou's followers; and on the holyday which Christians give to the divine worship, they often meet to adore the Garoudas, and feed them with meat. To kill one of them would be considered a crime equal to manslaughter. Siva's followers venerate the bull, which is sacred all over India. The serpent, too, especially the cobra capella, is held in great respect; temples are erected to these reptiles, and those which find their way into houses often receive sacrifices, and, what they prefer, food. But not content with adoring brute creatures, they make gods of rough stones. Frequently, in travelling through the country, one may perceive a number of rough stones arranged in a straight line or a circle by some devotee, who has rubbed them over with saffron; another takes it into his head to offer up a sacrifice of a cock or a lamb to these stones, and smears them over with the blood; this is sufficient to render these stones holy in the eyes of the neighbouring people, who immediately begin to worship them, and perhaps before long some rich native builds a temple on the spot. Such has been the origin

* 'Salam' is originally an Arabic word, and is a general word of salutation of the Mussulman population in India. The term is in some measure adopted by the Hindoos, and the way of offering it is different according to the caste of the person presenting it and the rank of the person receiving it.

of many of the most famous temples in India. Others have arisen from a suniassi, or penitent, affixing a rag of his clothes to a bush, in token of the holy emotion he felt accidentally in the spot; seeing this, others imitate his example, and soon the bush is counted sacred, and all hung with rags; a stone is placed before it, reddened with the juice of the betel-nut; perhaps a wall is built around; and if a rich man take a fancy to build a temple there, idle Brahmins will crowd to it, festivals will be held, and it becomes a celebrated place.

Many Europeans would willingly persuade themselves that all this is but symbolical, and that God is thus honoured in His works; but the testimony of the learned Brahmin Ramohun Roy should be conclusive to the contrary. He devoted much time to the study of Hindooism, in order to assist in the propagation of that Christianity which he cannot be said to have himself learned (since he died a Unitarian); but in his endeavours to convince his countrymen of the folly of idolatry, he showed the additions continually made by the Brahmins to their sacred books, and he testifies to their complete forgetfulness of all idea of one Supreme Being. He says they do not look on their idols as emblems of Him or His power, but firmly believe in the reality of their numberless gods and goddesses, all possessing complete and independent power; to make them propitious the temples are erected and the ceremonies performed, and it would be considered a heresy to think otherwise.

The morality of their sacred books is higher than would be supposed from the preceding sketch, and in several respects approaches to the Christian law. They require prayer, fasting, works of benevolence, patience in suffering. Frequent bathing, which in such a climate is necessary for health, is also enjoined. In the details which athing obligations of each caste are some wise regulations, mingled with much foolish superstition. Those who execute works useful to the public, such as tanks, temples, places of shelter for travellers, will be reckoned among the good and rewarded; those who burn with love and wisdom will go to the heaven of Brahma himself, and will share the delights of the gods. The wicked will endure indescribable torments: those who are disrespectful to their parents, or to the Brahmins, will burn in fire; calumniators and slanderers will be stretched on beds of red-hot iron, and forced to feed on ordure; the voluptuous, the indolent, and the hard-hearted will be cast into burning caverns, and trampled by elephants, who will feed on their flesh. But these torments, though of immense duration, will not be eternal; at length their bodies will be resuscitated, and they will live again, unless they have drunk of the water of the Ganges, which exempts from a fresh trial of this painful life. The reward of the good will never end.

They believe in the doctrine of metempsychosis; that is, the transmigration of souls. They think that, after more or less punishment, a soul will live again in a form suited to its deserts, rich or poor, of high or low caste, often even that of a beast; and therefore many of the natives will not destroy life in any shape. Before the introduction of this doctrine, there is no doubt that human sacrifices had been offered in all parts of India; now they show their devotion to their gods and goddesses by offerings of fruits and flowers, by performing works of penance or of usefulness to their fellow-creatures, and by celebrating splendid festivals in honour of their divinities. The magnificence of their temples, and the riches amassed in them, are perfectly astonishing. Among other ceremonies of their festivals, the idol is sometimes placed on an enormous car, and dragged in procession through the streets; and fanatics have frequently been known to throw themselves before this chariot, that they might be crushed under its wheels. This has, however, become rare of late years, in consequence of the active interference of the British Government, and the number of pilgrims has consequently very much diminished.

Europeans who think so much of the light and easy practices required or recommended by Catholicity to remind us of the sufferings of Christ, would hardly believe what the Hindoos endure in honour of their false gods. Some will, at certain festivals, allow themselves to be suspended from a height by iron hooks passed through the muscles of the back; others will walk on burning embers barefoot; some go almost or quite naked, wandering about, eating only enough to preserve life, and subsisting on alms; others have made a vow of silence; some travel about bearing Ganges water, others dancing and singing the praises of Vishnou; some penitents tear themselves with whips, or have themselves chained for life to the foot of a tree, or preserve for years some painful attitude, such as holding their arms raised above their heads so that they cannot feed themselves, or keeping the hands clenched till the nails have been known to grow out through the palm to the back. But it would be endless to relate the ingenious tortures which are practised by these unhappy creatures, and in which they glory, considering themselves happy beyond all others, and exalted by their performance. The custom of Suttee, or the burning of widows on the funeral-pile of their deceased husbands, need not here be alluded to, as the English Government make every effort to check it, and for many years it has ceased in the south of India, with which our Mission is principally interested. Of the frightful licentiousness authorised and encouraged under the name of religion, we will not speak; but this we may say, that nothing in the annals of heathen Greece or Rome, nothing among the practices of the early heretics, exceeded it.

A brief mention of the castes into which the Hindoos are well known to be divided may be interesting. The chief of these are the Brahmins, said to have sprung from the head of Brahma, and therefore superior to all others, and enjoying many privileges. They are considered the interpreters of the gods, and are the depositaries of all knowledge; but they usually lead a very idle and evil life. Many of them hold small civil appointments under the English Government, and they are certainly the cleverest and most intriguing race in India, but comparatively few of them have become Christians. The next caste is that of the Chatrias, or warriors, who are said to have sprung from the arms of Brahma; then the Vissias, labourers and merchants, who came from his body; and the Soudas, or artisans, from his feet. The names of the castes vary somewhat in different parts of the country: in Madura, the next to the Brahmins are the Moodeliars and Vellalers, and some of both castes have become Christians,—some of them even are among the most fervent. Their rank makes them very useful as an encouragement to others. After them come the Maravers, who are considered noble, and among whom many were converted by the early missionaries; but latterly the entire privation of spiritual instruction and aid, and the violence of evil passions, have made most of them relapse into idolatry. They are the robber caste—fierce and harsh. Their numbers have rapidly diminished, and they are not now a large caste, or by any means rich. The Odiages, or labourers, rank next, and are both numerous and wealthy. All these castes are subdivided, as the different names which one caste frequently bears will sufficiently indicate. The Soudras are the most numerous, and the subdivisions of this caste are endless. Every one is obliged to follow the calling of his father. Military service, commerce, agriculture, and weaving are honoured in all castes, and the first three trades may be followed even by Brahmins; while the Paria is not forbidden to weave. There are priests in every caste, as well as among the Brahmins. There are also many tribes not strictly counted as castes at all; the chief of these is the *outcast* tribe—called Paria: they form one-fourth of the whole population, and are almost universally looked down upon and shunned. Some think them the remains of a conquered nation, the original inhabitants of the country; but it is much more probable that they consist of persons whose ancestors were banished for crimes from the other castes. Some of them are intelligent, and contrive to amass considerable wealth: from amongst them Europeans take the greater number of their servants; which fact alone has immensely contributed to the prejudices of the higher castes against Europeans and their creed. The excessive humiliation to which they used to be subjected by the superior castes is wearing away rapidly. It would be impossible here to enter into the many minor details of these great divisions.

There are other religions beside Brahminism in India, as Bouddhism, the sect called Djaïnas, the followers of Nawik, and, finally, Mahommedanism. This last, the most numerous next to Brahminism in India, is too well known to need any notice here; but of the three others it may perhaps be interesting to say a few words.

Bouddha is said to have been born in the north of India, of the family of *Sakya*—one of the most noble of the Brahmin caste. Many wonders attended his birth, and prophets called him the God of gods. His wisdom and beauty were superhuman, and the people were never weary of listening to him. Touched at the woes of the human race, he withdrew to a desert, where he led so austere a life that his health suffered, and the milk of 500 cows was necessary to restore him. He then, at the request of the gods themselves, began to preach, overcame the five worshipers who opposed him, and spread his doctrines widely in India. They appear to be merely a reformation of Brahminism, from which Bouddhism differs principally in having a regular hierarchy, governed by a spiritual prince, in each country where it exists: it is sometimes a complete ecclesiastical empire—as, for instance, that of the Lamas of Thibet. The Brahmins violently opposed it, and between the third and seventh centuries of our era India was deluged with blood by the two sects, till at length the Bouddhists were driven from the country. Their creed, however, prevails widely in Thibet, China, &c., and in the Island of Ceylon. Some learned writers are much inclined to identify Bouddha with the early heresiarch Manes, who certainly took refuge in India during a portion of his career.

The sect of the Djaïnas appears also to be an attempt to bring back the religion of India to its original form; they reject with horror the Trimourti and all the fables connected with it, the worship of animals, and all the Brahminical superstitions. They believe in one Supreme Being, who is absorbed in the contemplation of his own perfections, and in no way interferes with this world; they believe matter to be eternal, and admit the metempsychosis, and the reward and punishment of men according to their actions, but without any intervention of the divinity. They never take food when the sun is below the horizon, and always have bells ringing or gongs sounding, to prevent their ears being polluted with the words of passers-by; they scrupulously clean their vegetables, lest they should destroy animal life. They have some well-endowed temples; one in the Mysore is in the centre of three mountains,—on the summit of one of them is a colossal statue of the celebrated penitent Goumatta, seventy feet high, sculptured out of a single piece of rock.

The religion of Nanuk is professed by the Sikhs. They too reject the Trimourti, and worship one Supreme Being, to whom they address their prayers directly. Warriors by profession, they nevertheless cultivate the earth and keep flocks.

There are also a few Parsees, followers of Zoroaster, scattered through the country of Southern India. In Bombay they are more numerous, and several of the richest merchants and most skilful tradesmen are of this race. Here and there a few thousand Jews are to be found in different parts of India.

Were it possible in this short sketch to dwell at greater length on this subject, it would be interesting to point out the extraordinary resemblances between Hindoo traditions and Scripture history; we find, disfigured by their wild idolatry, traces of the lives of Abraham, Moses, Job, Samson, and others; and several of the sacrifices have clearly been borrowed from the Jewish law. Some of their accounts of the creation and of the deluge strongly recall, and almost repeat, the words of the Book of Genesis. They speak of the first man and woman being created innocent and falling into sin, as also of an earthly paradise; the history of Chrishna, for instance, has a singular resemblance to that of Moses; but our space forbids us to pursue the parallel. The Hindoos are supposed to be descended from Shem,* though it is probable that the

* Some modern philologists, from new researches, are of opinion that the Hindoo race is descended from the same stock

race of Ham is mingled with them; and as Jews were certainly settled in India and China as early as three centuries before the Christian era, they might have borrowed much from them. We even find a distinct prophecy of an expected Saviour, containing the very name of Jesus, and certainly more ancient than the coming of our Lord. The great antiquity once attributed to Hindoo records, which carried them back far beyond the Mosaic era of the creation, has been distinctly disproved, and is now abandoned by all. Of the four yougarus, or periods, into which they divide their history, the first three are clearly fabulous, and are in fact so reckoned by themselves, as they date every thing from the commencement of the fourth, or iron age, in which we now live; it goes back to the period of the deluge, and agrees wonderfully with our common chronology, the difference being only sixty years. Many writers, whose acquaintance with this subject will not be questioned, declare that all the histories and antiquities of India confirm what is related in our Scriptures.

Although the preceding sketch of Hindoo mythology is taken from the most approved Brahminical records, it must not be imagined that this is commonly known or received amongst the people. Such Hindoo lore is now far less known and cared for than in former times. The great schools and centres of Brahminical learning have long since almost ceased to exist; very few read their ancient records, and still fewer care for what they contain. In a word, Paganism in all parts of India, but specially in the south, is an affair of usage, of custom, of routine; the people neither examine nor question about it, they simply accept it. Their forefathers were Pagans,—they are the same. Their religion is sim-

as the European, and belongs to the great family termed by them Indo-Germanic.

ply gross idolatry, with all its absurdities and aberrations. They neither examine, reason, nor reflect about it. A very small number of the most intellectual amongst them, whilst they observe all the exterior ceremonies, and follow the public in their idolatrous worship, admit a sort of universal Pantheism. In their ideas, every existing being is an emanation from the Universal or Essential Being, and must one day be reabsorbed by him. Every existing thing, then, partakes of the Divine nature.

The Pagan temples are still frequented by the people, and kept up by the priests on account of the great wealth they possess. The idolatrous festivals are still celebrated with very considerable pomp, and attract a large number of worshipers. Nevertheless, it is manifest to any one who has lived for some years in the country and watched what was going on around him, that the influence of Paganism is on the wane, and that it no longer possesses, especially in the south, where some of the most magnificent temples exist, the same empire and *prestige* over the minds of the people that it did in former times. There is a slow but irresistible work going on amongst the masses, which is gradually detaching them from their former ideas. As the English Government no longer allow the contributions to the temples, sanctioned by ancient custom, to be levied by force, these contributions rapidly diminish; and as attendance at the great Brahminical ceremonies can no longer be made compulsory, the affluence of the people to these festivals is much decreased. From these two reasons, the pomp and brilliancy of the old Pagan ceremonial is fading away, and the people are becoming comparatively indifferent to their religious festivals, which in some places are actually no longer celebrated, and have fallen into complete disuse. On the other hand, the number of Catholics is rapidly, and in some districts sensibly, increasing. Christian churches are rising in towns, in villages, and in hamlets, and their festivals are being celebrated with a degree of splendour unknown before, and with a concourse of people which strikes the oldest Pagans with surprise. Diverse Christian works of charity are being also gradually introduced into the country, and in their development command the esteem and attract the hearts of those who witness them. A Brahmin of the old school lately remarked, with a sigh, "Yes, we clearly see that the people are beginning to draw away from us; the true religion is spreading all around us; and we too shall have to yield in our turn." Thus Providence ordains that exterior circumstances should in so many ways contribute to favour the work of Divine Grace, and lead to the numerous conversions which are now annually taking place. How all-important is it for those who have the glory of God at heart to help forward this movement by their alms, deeds, and prayers!

CHAPTER III.

INTRODUCTION OF CHRISTIANITY INTO INDIA.

From the earliest Christian writers and traditions, we find that the apostle St. Thomas preached in India; on this point the testimony of St. Gregory Nazianzen, St. Jerome, Theodoret, and others, is quite clear; and the traces of Christianity found by the Portuguese confirm the fact. Among others, a plate of copper, engraved with half-obliterated letters, was dug up in 1543, and presented to Alphonsus de Sousa, the Portuguese governor. A learned Jew deciphered it as a donation from a king to the Apostle St. Thomas of land on which to build a church. When the foundations of the fortress of Goa were being dug, they discovered ruins of an old building, and among them a bronze cross, with a figure of our Saviour fastened on it. And what is yet more curious, in 1568 some Portuguese at Meliapore, wishing to build a chapel on a hill near the tower where tradition said the Apostle had been martyred by the Brahmins, they discovered in digging a white marble slab, two feet long by one six inches foot wide, on which was carved in relief a cross, whose four points were flowers. It was surmounted by a dove, which seemed to peck at the top of the cross. Around it was a triple arch, and beyond that were strange characters. The cross and the stone were stained with blood. After some time, a learned Brahmin was found, who read the inscription in the following words: "Since the Christian law appeared in the world, thirty years after the 21st of the month of December, the Apostle St. Thomas died at Meliapore, where there was a knowledge of God, and a change of law, and the destruction of the devil. God was born of the Virgin Mary, was obedient to her for the space of thirty years, and was God eternal. This God taught His law to twelve apostles, and one of them came to Meliapore with his staff in his hand, and built a church there; and the Kings of Malabar, and of Coromandel, and of Pandi, and of several other nations, willingly resolved, agreeing together, to submit themselves to the law of St. Thomas, a holy and penitent man. The time came when St. Thomas died by the hands of a Brahmin, and made a cross with his blood." Another Brahmin from a distant country gave a similar translation of it, without concert with the first. All this was attested at the time, and sent to Portugal to Cardinal Henry, afterwards king. In 1521 a sepulchre was found at Meliapore, containing bones and the head of a lance, part of an iron-shod stick, and an earthen vessel; the traditions of the place left little doubt that these were relics of the holy apostle. We dwell on these facts principally because they confirm what we have said above of the traces of Judaism and Christianity in the religion of the Hindoos; if Jews were settled in India three centuries before our era, and if St. Thomas preached Christianity there, it is easy to see how disfigured portions of Judaism and Christianity might have been mingled with the religion of the country.

There is every reason to believe the ancient traditions which assert the early preachings of St. Thomas, and the conversion of a large number of the inhabitants of several parts of India by this apostle. It is impossible to say at what time these first Christians disappeared, or when the faith planted by St. Thomas ceased to exist in the various places where he preached. It is, however, probable that Christianity was rooted out in the plains and open country during the wars of extermination between the Brahmins and Bouddhists during the first centuries of the Christian era. But in the hilly and mountainous districts, which now constitute a portion of the kingdoms of Travancore and Cochin, there are to this day a large number of Christians of the Syriac rite, whose very existence is one of the most curious phenomena of ecclesiastical history.

Lost in a maze of marsh and forest, and amidst the hills of Southern India, a population of 200,000 souls of Hindoo race have preserved the Christian faith without any communication with Europe, whilst all the surrounding and intervening nations have refused conversion or relapsed into heathenism. The traditions of these isolated Christians claim St. Thomas as their first teacher and apostle, and there is no reason to doubt it, for they evidently date from the preaching of the very earliest times. These early converts are called Nazareens, and to this day preserve that name, and form a distinct caste, which, by a wonderful providence of God, has preserved the essence of Christian faith in spirit and practice. Isolated from every Christian nation, and only able to keep up a very uncertain communication with the Patriarch of Babylon, whom they acknowledged as their ecclesiastical superior, they kept themselves free from all Pagan practices, and preserved a strictly Catholic belief in all those dogmas most disputed by Protestants, as, for instance, transubstantiation, auricular confession, purgatory, and the invocation of saints; and, what is still more remarkable, the celibacy of the clergy has been professedly observed amongst them. Unfortunately, however, through the influence of the bishops who were sent to them, they imbibed the errors of the Nestorians, admitting two separate persons in Jesus

Christ, when that heresy invaded the Eastern churches. In this state they were found by the Portuguese when they first landed in India,—affording thus a wonderful proof, which no cavilling can gainsay, of the antiquity and apostolicity of the main teachings of the Holy Catholic Church.

In 1599, at Diomper, on the Malabar coast, a council was held, presided over by the Archbishop of Goa, duly authorised from Rome. Archbishop Menezes, by prayer and exhortation, succeeded in convincing these Christians of the errors which they had inherited from Nestorius. By far the greater number gave their cordial submission to the Holy See, still preserving their own ancient Syriac rite and liturgy. Up to our own times they have persevered, and now form a population of over 200,000 souls. About 30,000 refused to abandon the errors of Nestorius, or to submit to the One, Catholic, and Apostolic Church. Some few years ago an effort was made to unite them to the Protestant Church. The first overtures were successful, as great worldly advantages were held out; but when they came to settle questions of doctrine, they found it impossible to abandon all their ancient faith, and the project was given up as hopeless.

After the settlement of the Portuguese in India, Goa was erected into an archbishopric, with several suffragan sees; but the progress of Christianity was very slight till the arrival of the great apostle of the Indies, St. Francis Xavier, one of the first associates of St. Ignatius, the founder of the Society of Jesus. He landed at Goa, May 6, 1542, and at once devoted himself to the reformation of the nominal Christians whom he found there; for so addicted had the majority of the Portuguese become to the acquisition of worldly riches, that they wholly neglected the duties imposed by their faith; while if any poor idolaters were convinced of the truth by the efforts of the few missionaries then in the country, they dared not embrace it, for fear of the oppression of the Pagans. St. Francis and his companions quickly changed the face of Goa; and having wonderfully revived religion there, they went to preach along the coast of the fisheries on the south-west extremity of the peninsula, where the inhabitants were so oppressed by their Mahommedan masters, that they had sought the help of the Portuguese, who came to their assistance: in gratitude for this aid, they willingly listened to Christian preachers. Almost the whole nation was converted by the wonderful zeal of St. Francis; and short as was his stay, the seeds he sowed continue to fructify to this day, notwithstanding the scarcity of religious teachers, and the many other difficulties with which Christianity in India has had to struggle. St. Francis also preached on the Travancore coast, which extends about thirty leagues: in a short time it was almost entirely Christian, and forty churches were built, surrounded by fervent congregations. Though deplorably neglected since, from many circumstances to be detailed hereafter, the majority of the inhabitants of this district are even now Christians. The career of St. Francis Xavier is too well known to every reader of the Saints' Lives, and to every one interested in the progress of Christianity among heathen nations, to need further mention here. It is enough to say that, finding so vast a field was open to him, and how readily the nations embraced the truth, he wrote repeatedly to Europe for more missionaries, and many joined him. Being Superior-General of the Missions of India, he could dispose of all who came out as he saw best, and direct their energies to work out the good which he had begun with such astonishing success. He attached himself chiefly to those countries which listened readily to his teaching. Once, when he was on the coast of the fisheries, he disappeared into the interior of the country for a week; and, on his return, said that those people were not yet fit for the kingdom of God,—nor was any thing more ever known of his excursion into the Madura district. At first there were none but Portuguese missioners in India; but gradually priests of other nations, and of various religious orders, came forward, and the progress of the faith was very rapid. Among these missioners were many Jesuits: in the reign of Louis XIV. of France, a great number of French Jesuits were sent out; they spread themselves over most parts of India and China, and established several Missions, which flourished till the destruction of the Society.

The object of the present memoir is to speak of the Mission of Madura, which was founded by F. Robert de Nobili, nephew of the celebrated Cardinal Bellarmin. Born in 1577, in Tuscany, of a distinguished family, he entered among the Jesuits at Naples; and while still a novice, the historian Orlandini, his master, foretold that he would do much to promote the glory of God in India, —for which he offered himself as soon as he had completed his studies. On reaching Goa, he was sent to the Malabar coast: thence he proceeded into the kingdom of Madura, where the king, an ally of the Portuguese, had allowed a Christian church to be built for the Paravas, who resorted there for traffic. F. Gonsalvo Fernandez, a most fervent and zealous missioner, had laboured there for fourteen years, but had not converted a single native of Madura. The contempt felt for the Portuguese, in consequence of their eating beef, drinking wine, and communicating with Parias, made the people fear to degrade themselves if they embraced their religion. F. de Nobili resolved to strike at the root of this obstacle. He said: "I will become as a Hindoo to save these Hindoos,"—following the example of St. Paul, and making himself all to all to win all to Christ. After several years of study and preparation, and with his superior's permission, he presented himself to the Brahmins, declaring, with strict truth, that he was not a Portuguese, or, as they called them, *Prangui*, but a Roman rajah—that is, a noble—and a Suniassi—that is, a penitent who has renounced the world and its enjoyments. The life to which he thus condemned himself was most severe: he could associate only with Brahmins; his whole food was milk, rice, herbs, and water, once in the day; his dress a long robe of yellowish cotton, covered with a surplice of the same; a white or red veil on his shoulders; a cylindrical cap on his head; and on his feet wooden soles, resting on props two inches high, and held on by a peg passing between the great toe and the next. To this he added a cord, the distinctive mark of the Brahmin and Rajah castes; but theirs consists of three threads only, while his had three of gold and two of silver, and supported a cross. He told them that the three golden threads denoted the Three Persons of the Blessed Trinity; the two silver ones, the body and soul of the adorable Human Nature of Christ; and the cross, His passion and death. He separated himself from F. Gonzales, and built a church and a house in the Brahmin quarter of the city, where he buried himself in prayer and solitude, never quitting his house, and allowing visits with great difficulty. Curiosity is a great stimulant; and to those who came to see him, his disciple used to answer that he was praying, or studying, or meditating on the Divine law; and when admission was at length obtained, the father was seen seated cross-legged, in Indian fashion, on a dais two feet high, covered with red cloth, and with a carpet and a fine mat before him. All saluted him by raising their joined hands above their heads, and bowing them to the ground,—even the noblest did this; and those who wished to become his disciples repeated it three times, and then went and stood behind him.

His very extensive learning, the purity and perfection with which he spoke Tamul, and his extensive acquaintance with Hindoo poetry and literature, delighted every one, and his fame spread widely. The king wished to see him; but as he did not think it yet time to appear in public, the reply was, that the Suniassi was absorbed in prayer and contemplation. It was taken for granted that he did not wish to go into the streets, lest he should sully his eyes by looking on women: so high was the idea of his chastity—a virtue the more admired by the Hindoos because so little practised.

But this vain reputation was not F. de Nobili's object; he aimed at the salvation of souls; and to succeed the better in this aim, he bound himself by vow to follow this new and painful life till his death. His first conquest was a Gourou, or priest, with whom he disputed four or five hours a day for twenty days. An abstract of this discussion would be both curious and interesting; but only a short account can be here given of his wonderful and most successful labours. Gradually disciples collected around him, and he instructed them in the Catechism, and tried them well before he granted them Baptism. Several among them were remarkable for their holy lives; and Albert, the Gourou above named, had great power over evil spirits, and became distinguished for his sanctity. *Possession** was common

* To this day the visible action of the Evil Spirit is by no means uncommon in India; and what reason is there to disbelieve the *present* existence of what we know on the authority of Scripture to have unquestionably existed formerly? If Christianity has diminished the power of the devil in Christian countries, we may naturally suppose that his power remains unbroken where the Cross has never been planted.

among the Hindoos, as may well be imagined from the lives they lead; and Albert cast out many demons, sometimes obliging them first to testify publicly to the truth of the doctrines preached by F. de Nobili; which made a great impression on the heathens. The good Father himself was also gifted with the power of healing miraculously; and during the time that he considered it conducive to the conversion of the heathens to remain secluded, he several times sent his reliquary by some of the converts to sick persons, who were healed at its touch.

After a time his great success excited the terror of the Pagans, and a persecution was raised against him; but he quietly continued his proceedings, availing himself of the protection of some powerful friends whom he had secured, and the storm passed away, as did others at different times. By degrees F. de Nobili showed himself more in public, as he found he could venture to do so without shocking the prejudices of those whom he wished to gain to Christ. In one of his letters we find the following account of his day. 1st, The usual exercises of the Society: that is, meditation, Holy Mass, self-examination, spiritual reading, Divine Office, &c. 2d, Study of the Sanscrit and Badage tongues, and of the Vedams, or Sacred Writings of the Hindoos. 3d, Composition of a large Catechism suited to the people. 4th, Four instructions daily to catechumens and to Christians. 5th, Audiences given to friends and to those curious to see him, in which he had to listen patiently to the most ridiculous tales. For forty-five years he led this life, converting immense numbers, and gradually associating other missioners in his labours. At one time a ridiculous report reached Europe that he had turned Pagan; and his uncle, Cardinal Bellarmin, wrote him a long letter to remonstrate with him against such a crime; to which he replied by showing the great influence he had gained by his way of life, and giving a full account of his motives, which entirely satisfied his holy and learned uncle.

F. de Nobili's reasons for thus adopting native customs, and mingling among the natives as one of themselves, have been much questioned, not only by Protestants, but even by Catholics, apparently incapable of understanding the difficulties he had to contend with, or of appreciating his success. The contrast between the uselessness of all the efforts of his holy and zealous predecessor, F. Gonzales, and the numerous converts made by him and those who trod in his footsteps, ought alone to be a sufficient reply; but when it is added that the good thus done has not been effaced by the long years of spiritual destitution which followed the destruction of the Society of Jesus, and that he acted throughout with the permission of his Bishop, we think every cavil must be silenced. So clear and forcible was his explanation, that it had great weight in inducing Pope Gregory XV., at a later period, to allow the converted Brahmins to retain certain caste distinctions and customs, which, though apparently superstitious, were by themselves looked upon merely as marks of their nobility. The indomitable pride of the Brahmins, which seems born with them, and nurtured from their earliest breath, has always been a great bar to their conversion. The system followed by F. de Nobili was the only method which ever met with success amongst them. Their dread of lowering themselves among their fellows by a change of religion, and being looked upon as Parias for associating with Europeans or Parias, was to most an insuperable barrier, which F. de Nobili removed in a great measure by the manner of life which he led. This distinction of castes, and the contempt felt by the members of the higher castes for all beneath them, is still a great hindrance to the spread of Christianity; so much so, that even catechists have been known to object to instruct those of a caste inferior to their own; and when native Hindoos have been educated and ordained at Rome, those of a higher caste have found it difficult to acknowledge their sacred character.

F. de Nobili and a few others laboured, as we have described, for five-and-forty years. The Mission was supported entirely by the resources spared with extreme difficulty by the establishments in the province of Malabar; for as Madura did not belong to Portugal, it received no funds from that country. The strict poverty practised by the missioners enabled four individuals to subsist on a sum calculated for only two: one was maintained by a small pension from his family; and two others by the rector of the college on the fishery coast; and by a house at Goa, with a little occasional help from the General of the Order. Had their resources been greater, could F. de Nobili have carried out his plan of establishing a college for Brahmin converts, and have been seconded by a greater number of missioners, perhaps Paganism might have been destroyed in Southern India. As it was, these hardworking missioners converted and baptised fully 100,000 idolaters. At length, sinking beneath his toils and privations, and nearly blind, F. de Nobili was recalled by his superiors, first to Jaffnapatam, and then to Meliapore, where he lived five years longer, exerting what strength and sight he had left in composing and dictating books in the native tongue for the assistance of his fellow-missioners.

Throughout his career he had been particularly devout to the Blessed Virgin, under whose protection he placed his mission. To spread this devotion among his converts, he composed Tamul verses in her praise. He died at Meliapore in 1656, aged eighty.

The loss which the Mission experienced in him was some years later compensated by the labours of F. John de Brito, a Portuguese Jesuit, son of a viceroy of Brazil, who chose the Madura Mission as the most laborious, and who toiled in it and in the neighbouring districts with almost incredible success. He may be called the founder of the Mission of Marava, and is supposed to have brought nearly 60,000 Hindoos to the faith. He had made many converts in the province of Marava, when the Prince Ranganadadeven forbade him, under pain of death, to remain in the country, or to preach to his subjects. He withdrew for the time, intending to return very shortly, as he could not resolve to abandon his converts, and looked on martyrdom as a great happiness. He was, however, ordered by his superiors to go to Europe as their Procurator-General, and he reached Lisbon in 1687. The King of Portugal endeavoured to detain him in Europe, but he replied that many were capable of filling the high posts offered him at home, but in Madura there were few missioners; and even if many should be willing to go thither, they had not the advantage of knowing the language and manners of the people as he did. On his return to Goa, he did not even wait to recover from a severe illness he had contracted on the voyage, but proceeded at once to all the Jesuit establishments in Madura, of which Mission he had been appointed visitor. He then went to Marava, where there were several churches scattered among the forests. The heathen priests soon put his life in such danger that he could not remain two days in one place without great risk; but the blessing granted by God to his labours in the baptism of 8000 converts supported and consoled him during the fifteen months which elapsed before his martyrdom. Prince Teriadeven, one of the principal lords of that country, which his ancestors had once ruled, was seized with a mortal disease, and reduced to extremity; finding no benefit from his false gods, he sent to beg F. de Brito either to come to him, or to send a catechist to teach him the doctrines of the Gospel; a catechist was sent, who repeated a portion of Scripture over him, and he was instantly cured. He again entreated F. de Brito to come to him, which the holy missioner ventured to do, and celebrated with him the Feast of the Epiphany, in company with 200 newly baptised converts. His zeal, his powerful preaching, and the joy displayed by the new Christians, so struck Teriadeven, that he begged to be baptised also; but F. de Brito told him he did not yet know the pure life required by Christianity, and that it would be a sin before God to baptise him till he was duly instructed and prepared. He then explained to him the Gospel law regarding marriage, which was very necessary, as Teriadeven had five wives, and a multitude of concubines. He answered, that this difficulty would soon be removed, and instantly went to his palace, summoned all his women, declared to them that he was resolved to spend the rest of his life in the service of so good and powerful a Master as the God of the Christians, and that, as His law forbade more than one wife, the others should receive a suitable maintenance, but he must separate from them entirely. They tried to move him by prayers and tears, but he was firm. His youngest wife, who was a niece of Ranganadadeven, went to her uncle with bitter complaints, in which she was supported by the heathen priests, who had long hated F. de Brito, because the number of his converts much lessened their income. They told the king that the greater part of the temples were abandoned, no sacrifices offered, no festivals held in them, and that they intended to withdraw from the kingdom, that they might not witness the vengeance which the offended gods would take on all who countenanced such wickedness. Ranganadadeven immediately ordered all the churches to be burned, all the houses of the Christians to be pillaged, and a heavy fine levied from all who persisted in this creed; which orders were so strictly obeyed, that many Christians were completely ruined. On the 8th January 1693, F. de Brito was seized, together with a Christian Brahmin, named John, and two boys, who would not leave him. Exhausted in health by the hardships of the twenty years he had spent in Madura, he was so weak that he fell repeatedly; but was forced by blows to rise and walk on, though his feet were bleeding and greatly swollen. At one village they were exposed for a day and a half to the mockeries of the people, placed on one of the idol cars; and before they reached the court a catechist, to whom F. de Brito had given charge of one of the churches, was added to their number. Prince Teriadeven succeeded for a time in lessening the harshness with which they were treated; but, notwithstanding his efforts, days passed in which no food was given them but a little milk once in the twenty-four hours. He also tried to induce Ranganadadeven to make some of his leading Brahmins dispute publicly with F. de Brito, but was answered by a command instantly to worship some idols which were in the room. He refused, saying he had lately been healed of a severe illness by the holy Gospel, and could not renounce it to the destruction of both soul and body. A young lord present, who had also been healed by F. de Brito, obeyed the king's command, and was instantly attacked again with his disease, so violently that he was soon at the point of death. He entreated to have a crucifix brought him, and cast himself before it, begging God's pardon for his sin. Hardly had he finished his prayer, when he found himself quite well. Ranganadadeven next had recourse to magic arts, to compass F. de Brito's death by the power of the gods; but he thrice repeated ceremonies which were believed all over the country to be inevitably fatal to any one against whom they were used, and of course they had no effect on the holy confessor. Another ceremonial, believed to be all-powerful over gods as well as men, was then tried, but equally in vain. Still the king and the Brahmins only repeated that F. de Brito was the most powerful enchanter ever seen, and they asked him if his Breviary, which had been taken from him, were not the source of his power, and whether it would save him from their muskets. They were just going to fire on him, when Teriadeven threw himself among the soldiers, and said he would die too if they killed his beloved master. He was so much respected that Ranganadadeven dared not persevere, but sent F. de Brito secretly to his brother, who lived at Orejour, a distance of two days' journey. His sufferings before he reached this town were frightful; for, as he was too weak to walk, he was literally dragged most of the way, and was fed on nothing but a little milk. Ouriardeven, the king's brother, first commanded him to heal him, for he was blind and paralytic; but F. de Brito replied that God alone could do this. He was kept in prison three days, almost without food, and at length was led to where a high post had been fixed in the ground. A great crowd soon collected. He was allowed time to pray in silence, and then he embraced and pardoned his executioners. They seized him, tore off his dress, and seeing his reliquary hanging by a string from his neck, and fancying it some charm, cut it off by a blow of the sword, which wounded him severely. They then tied a cord to his beard, fastening it round his waist, to bend his head forward, and were about to cut off his head, when two Christians rushed forward, and threw themselves at his feet, protesting they would die with him; they were dragged away, and the holy missioner's head struck off with a heavy hatchet, February 8th, 1693. To their astonishment, the body, though placed so as to bend forward, fell backward, and the almost severed head lay with the face upwards; they hastened to cut it off entirely, as well as his hands and feet; they then fastened the body to the post. The two Christians had their ears and noses cut off.

We have related the career and death of F. de Brito at some length, because his canonisation is now under consideration, and he was solemnly beatified by his Holiness Pope Pius IX. in 1853. He is well remembered even yet in this country; and there is great devotion towards him, and confidence in his power with Christ.

The next remarkable name which appears in the annals of the Mission is that of Father Bouchet, who was the founder and builder of the handsome church of Aöur, about 1690. Till his time the missioners had in general concealed themselves as much as possible, living completely among the natives, and following their customs. Even with the greatest precautions, they were afraid to enter any considerable village except by night. But F. Bouchet so endeared himself to the people, that he thought he might venture to build a finer church than had yet been attempted, and to serve it more openly. The church of Aöur stands in a large courtyard, the inner walls of which are painted, and ornamented at equal distances by high pillars, on which rests a cornice surrounding the building. The altar is at the intersection of the cross, and eight tall columns support an imperial crown, its sole ornament. Gold and azure abound in the inside, and the whole architecture is a mixture of European and Indian, which produces a very good effect. The church is under the invocation of the Blessed Virgin, and was much frequented as a pilgrimage. It is still a place of great resort, but is one of the many churches founded by the Jesuits, and served by them till the suppression of the Society, which is now in the hands of the Goanese clergy.

Experience, and the example of these Fathers, proved that missioners in the interior must practise the austerities displayed by the Hindoo penitents; and accordingly they dressed, as F. de Nobili had first done, in a piece of yellow cotton, with wooden sandals. They lived on rice boiled in water, with a few tasteless vegetables, and sometimes a little milk; they drank nothing but water, often muddy and bad, and slept on the bare ground, or at most on a tiger-skin spread on boards. They lived in mud cabins thatched with straw, which, in the rainy seasons, were often very damp; and their whole furniture consisted of a few earthen vessels, with palm-leaves for plates and dishes. God blessed their zeal; some of the princes granted them protection, and the people crowded to hear them and to be baptised. The fatigues they underwent, living on such bad food, are almost incredible. It was usual to prepare the Christians for each confession as if they had never made one before, by repeating for them detailed acts of faith, hope, charity, and contrition; and the numbers of penitents were often so great that the missioner could hardly find time to say his Breviary. Often troops of two and three hundred would come down, with their wives and children, having brought with them barely rice enough to support them on their journey, and allowed by their masters but a limited time of absence. The missioner was frequently obliged to spend the whole night hearing the confessions of the men, after having listened all day to the women, till, between want of sleep and want of proper food, he could hardly bring himself to eat when there was a moment to do so. The fervour of these poor Christians was most edifying; they would often travel two days' journey or more, to receive the Sacraments, and attend some religious festival: many of them perhaps might fall short of provisions before it was over, being very poor, and the richer ones would subscribe to purchase rice enough to enable them to reach their homes. The devotion displayed at these festivals was often most delightful to the missioner, who saw by it that his sacrifices and labours had not been in vain.

In the beginning of the last century the Jesuits had added to the Missions of Tanjore, Marava, and Madura, that of the Carnatic, which extended nearly 200 leagues in length, and contained sixteen flourishing congregations; there were also many Christians in Bengal, and in the dominions of the Great Mogul. The French Mission of Pondicherry alone numbered fully 60,000 native Christians, and was increasing daily; and without counting the northern districts, there were at least 1,200,000 Christians in the peninsula. Nor were these conversions ephemeral. The missioners, treading in the footsteps of St. Francis Xavier, spared neither time nor toil, and never baptised without ample preparation, and repeated entreaties on the part of the neophytes. The innocent lives of the Christians, and their firmness under persecution, showed them worthy of the graces they received. The change of life produced by baptism was truly wonderful, and so astonished the heathens, that they imagined the holy oils were some magic charm—so little could they comprehend such a complete alteration. Hereditary crimes were eradicated; converts from the robber castes ceased to steal; and missioners have declared that they have heard the confessions of whole villages of Christians without finding one individual guilty of a mortal sin. Their firmness under persecution was even more extraordinary, for the Hindoos are a cowardly people, and very accessible to flattery; but Christianity seemed to change their nature, and to inspire them with the most generous and heroic faith.

One instance of the fortitude displayed under persecution by a Christian convert is too remarkable to be omitted, though it was by no means a solitary case; but it is told in considerable detail in the letters of the missioners.

Nilen Pilley was of the Vellala caste, and born a heathen. His penetrating mind and his good qualities won the esteem of all who knew him, and he was very religious in his own way. God, who intended to call him to a knowledge of the truth, tried him with heavy losses, which grieved him the more because he was married. He had formed a friendship with a French officer, named Benedict Eustache de Lanoy, who, one day seeing him in very low spirits, spoke to him of the rapidity with which the goods of this world pass, and advised him to put his trust in the one true God, and he would find his melancholy vanish. Such conversations were frequently repeated, and the French officer explained the Christian faith to him. He reflected in the silence of night on all he learned, contrasting the perfections of the true God with the actions attributed to his false ones; and at length he told his friend he would become a Christian. Benedict de Lanoy sent him to F. Franzodi Buttari, an Italian priest, who then had charge of that portion of the district. The Father, fearing that his Pagan relations and the danger of losing his employment might prevent his perseverance, deferred baptising him; but the young convert so earnestly begged for it, protesting that, having once known the true God, he would rather lose fortune and life than abandon Him, that at length, after being taught all that was necessary, F. Franzodi baptised him under the name of Devasagayam, the Indian word for Lazarus.

Nilen immediately endeavoured to win his friends and relations also to Christianity. He first tried his wife, who considered Christians as degraded, because all classes of them worshiped the same God. Devasagayam reminded her that the same sun gave light to the highest and to the lowest castes, the rain fell on all alike, and they all trod on the same earth. Gradually he converted her, in spite of the eager remonstrances of her mother, who assured her that, if she became a Christian, no family of equal rank would marry her children. She was baptised under the name of Guanapou, which means "spiritual flower." He converted several of his relations afterwards; and the Brahmins, who were very much incensed at his opposing their false gods, waited their opportunity of punishing him. Father Franzodi wished to build a church, and Devasagayam went to one of the principal Brahmins about the court, and begged him to ask the king for leave to cut wood for this purpose. The Brahmin replied by violent threats; to which Devasagayam only answered, that he was ready to bear any thing they chose to inflict, and returned home, praying earnestly that God would give him courage and constancy. The Brahmins easily obtained an order to have him put to death, and soldiers were sent to seize him. He had already sent word of his danger to his friend Captain Benedict Eustache, who came and persuaded the soldiers to delay a little: meanwhile a priest came, and heard Devasagayam's confession, gave him the Holy Communion, and exhorted him to be courageous. As he was taken away by the soldiers, several persons met him, and said he had degraded himself by becoming a Christian; but if he would adore the gods of his forefathers, he might be restored to the king's favour. He replied, that he valued no honours but those never-ending ones promised by the King of heaven and of earth to His faithful followers. When the king heard this, he ordered him to be ironed and closely confined. Benedict sent a friend to comfort him; but the news reached the king's ears, and he sent a message to the officer, desiring him not to meddle with what did not concern him. Devasagayam continued praying earnestly that Christ would, through the merits of His sacred passion, enable him to suffer with courage.

Next day the king ordered him to be taken to a neighbouring forest, and there to have his head cut off; he also commanded that all who had become Christians should be persecuted. Some soldiers brought him word of the sentence, and he exclaimed: "I have long hoped for this happiness; your news is a source of great joy to me." On his way to the forest he was insulted by the country-people; but he answered cheerfully, and prayed as he went along.

A fresh order from the king commanded him to be cast again into prison, and he lamented the delay, fearing God did not think him worthy to suffer.

Soon afterwards the king directed that he should be led from village to village mounted on a bull, and struck with rods; that when he was all over wounds, he should be rubbed with pepper, which should also be put into his eyes, nose, and mouth; and that, when he was thirsty, he should have water from a cesspool to drink. This barbarous command was executed. Devasagayam repeated unceasingly the name of "Jesus," and bore his ever-renewed torments so heroically, that the people cried out it was a miracle; yet many insulted him. One day his guards left him for a short time, and a Christian stole quietly up to him, and read him our Lord's passion; when he came to the scourging at the pillar, Devasagayam stopped him, and, shedding many tears, exclaimed, that what he was enduring was not enough. Next day, as they were rubbing the pepper into his eyes, he said it was a good remedy for the sins committed by sight. Another day that the guards, either through pity or forgetfulness, omitted the pepper altogether, he reminded them of it; on which they tore his flesh again with blows, and left him in the hot sun, with only corrupted water to drink. He reflected on the gall our Saviour tasted, and swallowed it as if it had been perfectly pure.

He was then, by the king's command, kept in chains before the palace; but the Christians crowded to him to be healed of their diseases; and the king, enraged that a punishment he had inflicted to destroy Christianity only made it more known, had him removed to a distance and chained to a tree, where he was left without a roof to shelter him from sun or rain. His sufferings here were very great; but he was comforted and encouraged by a letter from Captain Benedict. After a time he was again removed, and a roof of palm-leaves given him.

The executioner of this district had no children, and had vainly offered numberless sacrifices to his gods to obtain them: hearing that many were cured by Devasagayam's prayers, he spoke to him on the subject, and was assured that he would have a son, which accordingly happened not long afterwards.

The martyr wept continually for his past sins. He had a tender devotion to the Blessed Virgin and St. Joseph; on one occasion they appeared to him in his sleep; and with them was our Lord, shining with light. Devasagayam awoke his companion; but the vision had disappeared, leaving only a brilliant light. The news of this vision spread about, and Christians and heathens crowded to see him. The king, enraged to find that all he did to degrade him only made him more honoured, had him removed again, and commanded that he should be left to die of hunger; but those who came to see him brought him food secretly. He also had the happiness of again going to confession and receiving the Holy Communion.

To terrify the Christians, the king next commanded that they should be stripped of their property. Many fled to another territory, and those who stayed, though grossly ill used, remained firm in their faith. Devasagayam was accused as being the cause of their obstinacy, and would have been beheaded, had not a Hindoo penitent, a great friend of the king's, represented that it was disgraceful to put a man to death for his religion; so his torments were renewed. One of the officers of his guard resolved to cut off his head; and the executioner, who had obtained a son by his prayers, warned him of it, and offered to help his escape. He wrote to consult Father Madrindram, the nearest missioner, who replied, that a soldier who had served his prince long would lose his reward if he were to fly at the moment of battle; and Devasagayam refused to escape, to the astonishment of the executioner. He was soon afterwards removed again, and once more chained to a tree, where he was left ten days without shelter. The Christians were forbidden to approach him, but the guards did not enforce the order.

Nearly three years had thus passed after his arrest, when the king gave a secret order for his execution. He learned it supernaturally, and took leave of his wife, begging that after his death she would go into another country, lest her relations should persuade her to apostatise, and promising that God would protect her if she were steadfast in her faith. He next made the sign of the cross over a sick girl who was brought to him, and healed her; and then prayed earnestly, till the soldiers came to take him to a solitary place and shoot him. He told them he knew what they intended, at which they were much surprised. Finding he could not walk as fast as they wished, they made him lie down, and passing a stick through the irons that fastened his hands and feet, carried him; which was excessively painful, as the irons wounded his limbs. On reaching the spot, he begged a few minutes to pray, which was granted, and they fired three muskets at him: he fell severely wounded, exclaiming "Jesus, save me!" and they fired again and killed him. They then withdrew, having taken off his irons and cast his body into a ditch. The Christians buried it in the church at Cottar, and many were cured by the earth stained with his blood. He was put to death on the 14th January 1752, seven years after his baptism.

The native Hindoo princes were not the only persecutors of the Holy Catholic faith: the Dutch settlers along the coast rivalled and even surpassed them in cruelty. On the coast of the fisheries, a Dutch preacher wished to persuade a Parava Christian chief that the faith he taught was superior to that the Paravas had received from St. Francis Xavier: the chief replied that he must prove it by working miracles at least equal or superior to those of the great Father; that he must raise a dozen dead to life, and heal all the sick. Force was then tried, but equally without success. Many endured scourges and tortures with the courage of the ancient martyrs, and their mothers rejoiced in their suffering thus for the sake of their Saviour. Children, when threatened with death, knelt down, and with clasped hands declared themselves glad to die for Christ. Many other converts suffered much from both rulers and relatives, and were sometimes obliged to give up all they possessed, and, carrying their children with them, seek a subsistence in some other place; yet persecution, sickness, and death they cheerfully accepted from the hands of their merciful God, rather than abandon His holy law.

These flourishing Missions had often much to suffer, first from the internal wars among the native princes, in which their undisciplined troops scattered themselves over the country and destroyed all before them, killing such of the inhabitants as had not hidden themselves in inaccessible places, and forcing the missioner to seek a refuge on the sea-coast, or in the mountains. On his return, he often found his church burned and his flock dispersed. All this became still worse when Europeans took part in these wars; the hatred they excited in those against whom they fought, and their conduct, so opposed to their religion, weakened the effect of its holy doctrines and morality; and the more the Europeans became known, the greater was the prejudice against Christianity, as being the creed they professed but did not practise. This aversion became so violent, that in some districts a heathen of good standing would not even venture to acknowledge an intimacy with Christians.

The controversy among the missioners themselves regarding what were called the Malabar rites was another circumstance which seriously checked the conversion of India. It is impossible for Europeans who have not lived in India to imagine the power of custom over the Hindoos; to them it is a supreme law, and all that goes against it is blamable and degrading. To oppose their customs would have been to alienate them entirely from Christianity, and most of the missioners therefore tolerated all such as were not clearly forbidden by the law of God or of nature. Persons ignorant of the country attacked these concessions fiercely, and in their accusations mingled with the customs permitted by the missioners to their neophytes many which they steadfastly opposed, as, for instance, the wearing of the *taly*, a jewel engraved with an idolatrous figure, worn round the neck by married women in token of marriage, like the wedding-ring in Europe.

In 1703 Cardinal de Tournon, Apostolic Legate in India and China, examined the question, and decided against the toleration of some of these customs; the Archbishop of Goa, the Bishop of St. Thomas, the Jesuit missioners, and others, appealed from this decree to Rome. Pope Clement XI. confirmed the decree temporarily, but appointed persons to examine the case more fully. It was long debated at Rome, and in 1727 Clement XII. repeated the confirmation of Cardinal de Tournon's decree. However, it was found impossible to observe it practically. A fresh examination took place, and some modification of it was permitted in 1734, allowing for a time the omission of some of the ceremonies in Baptism which were most offensive to Hindoo prejudice, such as the use of saliva, and the breathing in the child's face; recommending, but not obliging, the missioners to give the name of some saint to those they baptised, and requiring them to observe, as far as possible, the regulations of the Council of Trent regarding marriages. Some of the ceremonials to which the Hindoos clung were prohibited, but others were allowed, and no penalties of censure were attached to this brief. The missioners in general received it with joy, but some thought it did not sufficiently take native prejudices into consideration, and sent fresh petitions to Rome; however, in 1739, Pope Clement by a brief required from every missioner in the country, or who should hereafter go thither, an oath of obedience to this decision, and it was cheerfully taken. Benedict XIV., his successor, published a bull containing a complete history of the discussion, confirming the brief of Clement XII., and ordering that any missioner who would not obey it should be sent back to Europe. The Jesuits at once accepted this bull; they had always opposed the wearing the *taly*, and introduced instead a trinket engraved on each side with a cross, and fastened with a particoloured string of an indefinite number of threads, instead of the yellow cord of 108 threads worn by the heathens. To prevent superstitious customs at weddings, they obliged a catechist to attend them, accompanied by a Christian Brahmin, to see that our holy law was observed; but finding the horror of the Hindoos for the use of saliva and breathing in the christening ceremonies, they, with due sanction of the Bishops, continued to dispense with them. The greatest difficulty was about the Parias. To have any intercourse with them, and especially to visit them in their huts, was to become an object of hatred to all other castes, who would not afterwards accept any service from a missioner who had done so. After vainly endeavouring to overcome this prejudice, it was proposed to Benedict XIV. that there should be a separate class of missioners for these poor creatures, which was approved, and some of the Fathers at once devoted themselves to this painful duty, separating themselves entirely even from their brethren in the same country, and enduring all the privations imposed on this outcast class. One missioner would be seen moving about on horseback, or in a palanquin, eating rice dressed by Brahmins, and saluting no one as he went along; another, covered with rags, walked on foot, surrounded by beggars, and prostrated himself as his brother missioner passed, covering his mouth, lest his breath should infect the teacher of the great.

This extraordinary measure succeeded for a time, but it has now been entirely discontinued, as no longer essential. Sincere indeed must have been the honesty of purpose, and admirable the spirit of self-devotion, which could prompt a man of education and rank to become thus the apostle of the outcast, and to cut himself off entirely from the only human consolation which remained to him in his exile—the sweet converse and company of his fellow-labourers and brothers in Christ! The outburst of long-suppressed love and affection in the earnest embrace of two early friends and near relatives who met privately after months of separation as Brahmin and Paria missioner, is beautifully described in one of the early letters from the missioners.

One of the most remarkable labourers in this painful Mission was F. Artaud, who has been called the Apostle of the Parias. He used to collect them in a courtyard near the church, and instruct them unweariedly; they would sit around cross-legged, and listen with eagerness; not a week passed in which he did not win seven or eight, and often a far greater number, to the fold of Christ. In 1748 it is estimated that there were at least 385,000 Christians in the eastern part of the Indian peninsula, and a greater number on the western side, besides several flourishing Missions in the north of Hindostan, whence the faith was rapidly spreading over all parts of the country. The Island of Ceylon was so completely Christian when the Dutch Protestants took possession of it in 1650, that all their cruel persecutions could not eradicate it, though *they actually sent to the mainland for idolatrous priests to reëstablish Bouddhism*, and prohibited the landing of any Catholic missioner.

Yet the faith was so rooted in the hearts of the people, that after 145 years of persecution it still lingered, like fire beneath ashes, to burst forth brilliantly when priests could again appear.

The holy faith of Christ seemed likely in some years to triumph also in India; each year the progress was more rapid and decided. Christianity had laid powerful hold on many districts in the country, and, breathing its spirit into the patriarchal customs of the Hindoos, was producing a simplicity and holiness of life never perhaps surpassed, except in "the reductions of Paraguay." The European Fathers, by following up the severe manner of life by which the first successes of their predecessors had been obtained, were rapidly increasing the number of converts, and spreading the influence of the holy law of Christ; and as each one sank to the sleep of death, hastened by his heavy toil and voluntarily imposed austerities, he prayed for the nation to which his life had been given, and hoped that his successors would finish and accomplish the good work so dear to his soul.

Unexpected and sudden as the typhoon of the eastern seas, came the storm by which Divine Providence allowed these glorious hopes, these holy aspirations, to be for a time checked and baffled. The iniquitous policy of Pombal had prevailed in Portugal; the Jesuits were to be suppressed throughout the vast foreign possessions of that country as well as at home. The decree had gone forth. Sealed orders, to be opened by each distant governor at a certain hour on a fixed day, and put in execution on pain of death, were travelling to their destination. The Jesuits at home were lulled into security by an apparent diminution of the storm so long raging against them. Their brethren in the foreign Missions continued their holy labour of love without much further indication of their danger than what was intimated by letters from Europe, or by the cessation of those alms from home which enabled them to live and labour. At the same time and day, all over the world, wherever a Jesuit Father was within reach of a Portuguese official, he was rudely seized, loaded with chains, and cast into prison, to be sent off to Portugal by the first ship available.

The storm of infidelity, or, to use the expression of the author of *Christian Missions*, "that great outburst of blasphemy and crime which began with the suppression of the Jesuits and culminated in the French Revolution," was to have its victims, and the Jesuits were to suffer. "One hundred and twenty-seven Jesuits," continues Marshall, "were seized at once and cast into prison at Goa. A few weeks later, on the 2d of December, they were dragged on board a vessel, of which the captain vainly declared that from forty to fifty was the extreme number he could receive. But the orders of the viceroy, Count d'Ega, were imperative, and the ship started on a voyage during which twenty-four of the Fathers died of scurvy, and the rest arrived, more dead than alive, at Lisbon; where they were flung into dungeons, of which only the lowest and darkest cells were assigned for their dwelling. Here they languished for years, meek and resigned, in the midst of almost intolerable sufferings, and mourning rather for their orphaned flocks than for their own unmerited wrongs. Once they met during their captivity, each standing at the door of his cell, to hear from the mouth of a gaoler —fitting deputy and agent of the Marquis de Pombal— the total suppression of the Society. Thirty-five died in prison during the first sixteen years; among whom were Diaz, Albuquerque, and Da Silva. And when at length the doors were opened, and they were permitted to reënter a world in which they had no longer a home, a family, or a calling, forty-five Fathers survived; sole remnant of all the missionaries of India, China, and America, amounting to many thousands."

The Mission of Madura was, however, not destined thus hopelessly to perish. Some few escaped the first swoop of Pombal's agents, and lived on for some years in the country till they reached the term of their apostolic life. One only, Father Andrea, lived till 1816, and heard the joyful news of the restoration of the Society of Jesus; and some fifteen years later, with their zeal and courage as earnest as ever, the children of St. Ignatius returned to the widowed Mission of Madura. How well and successfully they have laboured will be seen in the following chapters.

CHAPTER IV.

SHORT NOTICE OF PROTESTANTISM IN SOUTHERN INDIA.

In giving an account of the labours of the Catholic missioner in India, it would seem, at first sight, scarcely relevant or necessary to enter upon the subject of Protestantism. However, the Jesuit in Southern India, having devoted his life to the preaching of the Gospel of Christ crucified, finds himself, amongst other difficulties, in presence of the many sects of Protestants who of late years have overrun the peninsula of Hindostan in large numbers, distributing Bibles and tracts in thousands, and spending gold and silver in handfuls, in order to make proselytes to their varied forms of Christianity. On the side of the Protestant missionary have been worldly influence, immense resources, and often much industry and effort, especially on their first arrival in the country. The works written and edited in Tamul — the language of Southern India—by some of the Protestant missionaries show also that there has been no small amount of talent amongst some of them. Thus all that man, unaided by the grace of God, could bring, has been for a long time, with persevering human effort, brought to bear upon the masses of Hindoo Pagans. As the very soul and existence of Protestantism is its active opposition to Catholic doctrine, its establishment and spread in India has in no small degree increased the difficulties of the Catholic missioner, who, in his poverty and isolation, has had to struggle single-handed against the united efforts and wealth of the divers Protestant sects, which, in all their variations of doctrine, agree only in the condemnation of Catholicity, and in their effort to place it on a level with Paganism in their preachings and writings.*

The usual means employed by the Protestant missionaries were—firstly, the spreading of Bibles in immense numbers through the country; secondly, the dissemination of misrepresentations of Catholic doctrine, in pamphlets and tracts, as well as by word of mouth; thirdly, the regular salarying of a certain number of converts; fourthly and lastly, though by far the most important, the establishment of large numbers of schools, of all sorts and sizes, in which the teaching was not only gratuitous, but the scholars were even paid for attending. The immense sums of money put at the disposal of the various societies by the liberality of the people of England and of America enabled them to carry out all their undertakings regardless of expense, and provide themselves with every human appliance that money could command. The result, when compared with the means employed, has been a signal failure. To the Catholic mind this failure is easily explained; for the truth of God cannot contradict itself in one single tittle, and cannot therefore exist amongst diversity of doctrine. The Catholic knows also that the grace of God is inseparable from His truth, and "His grace alone" can save the souls of men. There has been no permanence in the Protestant successes. Jaffna in Ceylon, Tranquebar, Tanjore, and Tinevelly have successively been held up in the last forty years on the different platforms of public meetings, and their past successes and bright prospects for the future described in the most glowing colours. The fine establishments which actually existed

* Some years ago a large sum of money was offered as a premium, at Calcutta, for the best essay, written by a native, to prove "the identity of Romanism and Heathenism."

in those places are no longer a source of congratulation; the vast sums of money expended have left no adequate trace behind; and the brilliant promises, which have so often thrilled with hopeful enthusiasm the hearts of those who attended "the May Meetings" at home, have never been practically realised.

This failure is only the more striking in proportion to the extent of the means used in trying to establish and develop these missions; and those of our readers who would wish to enter more fully into this subject, will find what is here alluded to amply supported by a succession of Protestant testimonies, collected from various sources by Mr. T. W. Marshall, in his work on *Christian Missions.*

CHAPTER V.

HISTORY OF THE NEW MISSION OF MADURA, AND OF THE INDO-PORTUGUESE SCHISM.

THE source which principally supplied India with missioners was suddenly to be dried up: in 1773 the Society of Jesus was suppressed by a brief of Clement XIV. The Carnatic Mission was then intrusted to the Bishop of Tabraca and the Seminary of Paris. The Fathers of the Society who were then on the Mission continued the good work they had begun, and deeply as they regretted their own superiors, they punctually obeyed those now assigned to them by Providence, looking on the new missioners sent to India as beloved brothers and fellow-labourers. Most of the remaining Jesuits were old men, who had toiled for years among the natives, who looked upon them with the greatest respect. Had we space, a sketch of their labours would be most interesting; but we must proceed with our narrative. F. Mosac, the Superior of the Mission, gave way at once to the Bishop of Tabraca, by whom he was superseded after forty years of labour, during which he had baptised above 40,000 persons, chiefly sick children. He lived but a short time longer, occupied in prayer and the exercises of an interior life. The new and the old missioners worked on harmoniously, till the great French Revolution destroyed the Seminary for Foreign Missions at Paris; and for many years afterwards the Christians of India were left with but very few priests. In 1802 the French Missions in that country had but fifteen European clergymen, besides the Bishop, and most of these were aged, and too weak to penetrate into the interior of the country. They were assisted by four native priests. The Mission was divided into ten districts, several of the more inland of which had but one priest, who, though perpetually travelling from place to place, could scarcely visit each congregation of his scattered flock once in a year.

In 1817 there were but five or six aged European priests, and a Vicar-Apostolic, in the whole of this Mission; there was a little college at Pondicherry, where from time to time a few native priests were ordained. Some years after, the establishment for Foreign Missions sent a few clergy out to Southern India, and in 1824 there were fifteen priests; but many of them were old; and had they been in the most vigorous health, they could have done but little among so many Christians, scattered over such an immense extent of country. The Vicar-Apostolic wrote most pressingly for a supply of missioners, stating that there were congregations of three or four thousand souls who saw a priest but once in two years, and that even those who had a missioner living amongst them were very insufficiently attended; for what could one man do among seven or eight thousand souls, scattered sometimes upwards of thirty-five miles apart?

Whilst the Mission of the Carnatic was intrusted to the clergy of the "Foreign Missions" of Paris, the Madura Mission was made over for the time to the Indo-Portuguese clergy, of whom more will be said presently.

In 1830 the Vicar-Apostolic had the grief of seeing some Christian families, which had long vainly implored to have French or Jesuit missioners sent to them, and who, from the impossibility of otherwise attending to them, had been intrusted to the priests of a neighbouring district, give themselves up to the Protestants. In 1836 Mgr. d'Halicarnasse, who had toiled for forty-seven years in this Mission, and which he had governed as Vicar-Apostolic for twenty-two years, got M. Bonnand, Bishop of Drusipare, appointed his coadjutor, and soon afterwards died. There were then but sixteen priests in the whole Mission of Pondicherry. The Congregation of Foreign Missions, which has to supply five large countries in the East, found it so impossible to procure priests enough for Madura, that the proposal of the Propaganda to send Jesuits there again was gladly accepted. In 1837 four members of the Society reached Pondicherry, and five more followed during the two subsequent years. Spread over the interior of the country, they at once endeavoured, under the guidance of Mgr. de Drusipare, to revive the old Christian congregations. By a brief of 1836, various vicariates were established in Asia, according to the wants of the different countries. The Island of Ceylon was erected into a separate vicariate-apostolic: Madura, Tanjore, Marava, and the Mysore were committed to the charge of Mgr. Drusipare, as Vicar-Apostolic of the Coromandel Coast; the former diocese of St. Thomas, or Meliapore, was annexed to the vicariate-apostolic of Madras; the ancient dioceses of Cranganor and Cochin to that of Malabar; and authority over all these was given to the Vicar-Apostolic of Verapoly; Malacca, and the country beyond the Ganges, were subjected to the vicariate-apostolic of Ava and Pegu, and another vicariate was established at Bombay; Calcutta was also made a separate episcopal charge, and some few years later was made an Archbishop's vicariate, Dr. Carew being raised to that dignity. To these we must add the Archbishop of Goa, formerly Primate of the Indies, whose diocese has been narrowed to the small limit of the Portuguese possessions. These arrangements of the Holy See have been disputed by certain Portuguese and Indo-Portuguese priests, who, themselves unable to manage this immense country, could not bear to see it transferred to other hands.

To understand the state of things in this respect, to explain the opposition of Portugal and those influenced by her to the new arrangements of the Pope,—to describe, in short, what is called the Goa schism, which so miserably checked the progress of religion in India for many years past,—it is necessary here to give a slight sketch of what may be called the political history of Christianity in India.

Among the Portuguese navigators who found their way to Hindostan by sea in the fifteenth century were many knights of the Order of Christ, one of the military-religious orders instituted to fight against Mahommedanism. Many persons then thought that an attack made on those Eastern countries whence Islamism derived its strength would, by creating a diversion, much benefit those who were endeavouring to drive it from Europe; and with this view these knights joined in the voyage of discovery set on foot by the Infant Don Henry of Portugal, their Grand-Master. To them, for the protection of Christianity, the first attributions of Indian territory were made by the Holy See, and not to the Portuguese king or nation. In those times, the idea of taking possession of a newly discovered country by planting the national flag had not arisen, and all Europe considered the Pope as the arbitrator of differences, and as having supreme spiritual authority in the whole world. In the first grants, made later on by successive Popes to the Portuguese crown of all the territory they might conquer in India, no mention whatever was made of the right of patronage, as it is called, which has been so fertile a source of some good and of great evil. Portugal was, however, authorised to build churches and monasteries in the countries she conquered, and to send missioners thither. Leo X. was the first Pope who granted any right of patronage in these Eastern countries; but he attached to it, as a condition, that Christianity should be maintained and protected by the government; at the same time the right of advowson was limited to those districts of which Portugal then was, or might afterwards be, actually possessed. On these terms, four bishoprics were, at different times, erected in Hindostan, and in 1557 Goa, the chief seat of Portuguese power, was erected into an archbishopric, to which the others were made suffragans. The kings of Portugal very soon tried to claim under these grants far more extensive rights than had been intended by the Sovereign Pontiffs, and Urban VIII. refused to acknowledge the influence which they claimed to have over the nomination of Bishops-suffragan to Manilla, and also over the Bishops and Vicars-Apostolic sent to Japan in 1646, and afterwards to China. Portugal not only protested vehemently against this resistance to her aggressions, but ordered the governor of Macao, under pain of death, to let no one enter China who did not come from Portugal, and closed the African Missions in the same manner. In this extremity, the power of nomination to the sees of Cranganor and Cochin was yielded to the King of Portugal, though both places were under Dutch rule. Alexander VIII. extended the grant to the bishoprics of Pekin and Nankin in China; but it gave rise to such disorders, that in 1696 Innocent XII. dismembered these dioceses, to establish more solidly the authority of Vicars-Apostolic; and the resistance of Portugal to the change was vain. As for the episcopal sees in India, they were placed under the patronage of the Portuguese crown only on condition that they should be regularly endowed by the king in the districts of which he was master.

The Holy See never gave up the right of modifying

the limits of these dioceses, or making all necessary changes, whether they continued to be under Portuguese dominion or not, as we find in the brief issued by Clement X. in 1673, *Solicitudo pastoralis*, and also in the words contained in the brief for the erection of each see: "*Jus patronatus ex meris fundationi et dotationi competere*"—"The right of patronage arises solely from foundation and endowment."

It is therefore evident, that in reducing the extent of these ancient bishoprics, and even in suppressing them, the Holy See acted with uprightness and justice, whilst the opposition on the part of the Portuguese crown had lost all semblance of reason. For not only had Portugal entirely ceased to afford assistance and protection to the Catholic Missions in India, but had, moreover, seized upon and confiscated all ecclesiastical and Mission property within their reach. In 1836 the Vicar-Apostolic of Verapoly writes: "Since the change of government, the Court of Lisbon has ordered the magistrate last sent out to Goa not to give a farthing to ministers of the Gospel employed beyond the Portuguese territory; we may therefore feel assured that all pretensions to the right of patronage over the sees of Cochin, Cranganor, and Meliapore is abandoned." "For a long time," he adds, "there have been no Portuguese Bishops at Goa, at Cranganor, at Cochin, or at Meliapore;" and concludes with Cardinal Fornari, in accordance with most doctors of canon law, that "when the cause for which the patronage was granted has ceased, the right of patronage ceases also."

The Holy See, however, hesitated to exercise its undoubted right, and in 1832 Cardinal Pedicini, Prefect of the Propaganda, presented a request to the Portuguese ambassador that his sovereign would either fulfil the obligations undertaken with regard to the Indian bishoprics, or would renounce pretensions which put a stop to all good in that country, and rendered ecclesiastical government impossible. He pointed out that Portugal now possessed nothing but Goa, and that of all its former territories nothing remained but the claim of patronage, *which it could not exercise.* He therefore suggested that the Portuguese sovereign should name a new Archbishop of Goa, and that the other Sees should in future be considered as ordinary Foreign Missions. Still nothing was done till Gregory XVI. determined to act decisively, and began by erecting, with the consent and approbation of the English Government, vicariates-apostolic at Calcutta and at Madras, in 1834. Great opposition was made to this by Portugal; but the salvation of too many souls was at stake to allow any yielding on the part of Rome to claims so unreasonable. The Portuguese clergy seemed to have long acted on the principle, that it was better to let the people perish for want of religious aid, than to see them receive it from *Turkish Bishops*, as they called the Vicars-Apostolic, whose titles were taken from extinct sees in Asia Minor. They now strove to call in the help of the secular power and of the English Government, to check the execution of the Papal decrees.

In 1836 the Sacred Congregation met to find means of remedying such abuses, and the celebrated brief, *Multa Præclarè*, was carefully prepared; and meantime two more vicariates-apostolic, at Ceylon and Madura, were created. To the latter no nomination was immediately made, and its administration was temporarily committed to Mgr. Bonnand, Vicar-Apostolic of the Coromandel Coast. In 1838 a special decree annexed the old diocese of Meliapore to the vicariate-apostolic of Madras, and the dioceses of Cranganor and Cochin to the vicariate of Verapoly, on the Malabar coast. The Archbishopric of Goa had then been so long vacant, that the Portuguese clergy in India, having no one to recruit their numbers by fresh ordinations, were gradually becoming extinct, when unfortunately Portugal, aroused from its long apathy, and pretending to enter into the views of the Holy See, demanded canonical institution of a new Archbishop of Goa, who, however, made a solemn promise to the Roman Legate at Lisbón that he would submit to the arrangements of the brief *Multa Præclarè*. No sooner had he reached Hindostan than he confirmed all that the Goa clergy had done to oppose the new Vicars-Apostolic of British India. He even went further, and availing himself of some words inserted in his Bull of Institution, to which he gave an explanation completely at variance with the intentions of the Holy See, he claimed all the rights of his predecessors, as Primate of India, notwithstanding a brief which accompanied the Bull, and by which the Pope commanded him to respect the jurisdiction of the Vicars-Apostolic.

He immediately ordained an immense number of clergy of all grades, taken from every rank of life; many of them quite uneducated, and but few in any degree competent for the ministry. This step insured a long continuance of the nearly extinct schism caused by the previous opposition of the clergy of Portuguese origin to the establishment of the Vicars-Apostolic. The Archbishop also encouraged the intrusive Bishop-elect of Meliapore, nominated by Portugal, but rejected by Rome, and never consecrated. Moreover, the Bishop proceeded soon after to the visitation of his assumed diocese, and by so doing gave occasion to serious disturbances in many places. It is needless to point out the bad impression which all this made on the heathen portion of the Hindoos, or its still more deplorable effects on the Christians, who could hardly comprehend the point in question, which was one of discipline, not of doctrine.

The Holy See found severe cause of complaint against the Archbishop of Goa for his singularly arbitrary and uncanonical conduct. He was, in consequence, recalled to Europe; and, having apologised for, and in some degree repaired, the scandal he had given, he was nominated coadjutor to the Archbishop of Braga, and soon after died in sentiments of sincere repentance.

During all this time negotiations were pending between the Holy See and the Court of Portugal; and Mgr., now Cardinal, de Pietro was appointed by Rome, and sent to Lisbon to draw up a new Concordat. After long discussions and difficulties, this Concordat was signed at Lisbon, February 21st, 1857; but on account of fresh difficulties occasioned by the impracticability of the Portuguese officials, the ratifications were only exchanged in 1859; and it was not till the following year that its existence was officially notified to the Vicars-Apostolic in India. Though in many respects contrary to their opinions, and their repeated solicitations; though it seemed to put an end to all their dearest hopes of success in the object for which they had undertaken a life of toil and privation in the burning climate of India, this Concordat was immediately published by the Vicars-Apostolic. It was the will of Rome; that was sufficient for them. It is useless to enter into a full detail of this document; the more so, as the constant difficulties raised by the Portuguese, as to its bearings and purport, as well as their complete inability to fulfil its conditions, make it daily less and less likely ever to be fully carried out. In brief, its principal provisions were:

1. Arrangements for the nomination of a new Archbishop of Goa, and a definition of his diocese and of his jurisdiction.

2. Stipulations for the erection of fresh bishoprics for Portuguese Bishops in the former Portuguese (now British) territories in India, amongst which, in particular, were named Meliapore (or Madras), Cochin, and Malacca (all British possessions); and with them, in the same category, was named Macao, a strictly Portuguese colonial settlement.

3. Power was granted to the Portuguese Government, gradually, and in course of time, when it should suit their ability and wish, to define and establish new bishoprics for Portuguese Bishops over sundry other portions of British India; thus gradually empowering a future Portuguese hierarchy to supersede and displace the Vicars-Apostolic, and absorb their vicariates on certain conditions.

4. Six years were granted to Portugal to define and determine the means at her disposal to effect these changes and carry out these conditions; and during this time an extraordinary jurisdiction was granted to the Archbishop of Goa over all those churches and clergy who, at the date of signature, were still in open resistance to the Vicars-Apostolic in whose vicariates their churches were situated.

Portugal was thus gradually to assume the right of establishing an exclusively Portuguese hierarchy over the greater part of British India, of supporting the sees, and filling them with Portuguese subjects, to the virtual exclusion of all other ecclesiastics, British subjects included. The Portuguese diplomatists at Rome repeatedly asserted that these arrangements were a matter of such complete indifference to the British Government, that, though perfectly cognisant of them, no sort of opposition or disapprobation was expressed.

At the commencement of the year 1863 the Vicars-Apostolic announced the new order of things to their flocks, and the peace thus made with the Goanese schismatics.

The adherents of Portugal, on the other hand, considered this Concordat as a real triumph for their party; whilst the Vicars-Apostolic, who understood the serious detriment which the full execution of the Concordat would probably cause to religion, consoled themselves with the hope that in some way Providence would hear their earnest prayers, and interpose a remedy to the impending evil.

In the mean time the Apostolic and Portuguese Commissaries commenced their labours; and each succeeding conference showed more and more clearly that Portugal was determined only to execute such portions of the Concordat as were for her own advantage, and to ignore the rest.

The Apostolic Commissaries soon became most painfully impressed with the ignorance, incapacity, and venality of the Indo-Portuguese clergy. Change of climate and disappointment weighed too heavily on a constitution already enfeebled by years, and the Right Rev. Commissary died at the Neilgherry Hills, in the month of May, whither he had gone for change of air and rest, heartbroken at the hopeless task before him. As soon as this news reached Rome, his secretary, and his assessor Mgr. Howard, as well as a French missioner of experience, Father Despommiers, since consecrated Vicar-Apostolic of Coimbatour, who had been named second assessor to the Apostolic Commissary, were all called to Rome, to explain what had taken place. They were the bearers of petitions and letters from the Vicars-Apostolic, and even from the laity of the various congregations, which threw much light on the state of things, and showed how very incorrect were the representations of Portugal, in consequence of which the Concordat had been granted.

Immediately after their return, the Holy Father ordered a detailed account of the whole affair to be drawn up and presented to him. This was submitted to a special council of Cardinals to report upon. After mature consideration, the council met in June 1864. The Pope himself presided. The result has not been officially published; but, at all events, no further steps have been taken in carrying out a Concordat which now seems tacitly to be considered impossible. The prevailing opinion seems to be that his Holiness will soon establish a regular ecclesiastical hierarchy in India, in accordance with the present political and religious position of the country. A step which has been the cause of so much peace and profit to the Catholic churches in England and Holland cannot be without its good effect in India. Such a measure, if resisted by the existing Goanese priests in India, may cause trouble for a time, but must eventually lead to peace and order.

CHAPTER VI.

DAILY LIFE AND JOURNEYS OF THE MISSIONERS—CONSEQUENT MORTALITY AMONGST THEM.

In imitation of the great Apostle St. Paul, and following in the steps of Father de Nobili, the founder of the Mission of Madura, it is the daily effort of the Fathers, who are there striving to gain souls to Christ, to make themselves "all to all." The same zeal which has made the Catholic missioner adopt the hard and wandering life of the savage in order to convert him to Christ, has inspired the Jesuit in India to make himself an Indian. Rice and water must replace the bread which was his daily food in civilised life; liquor he must never touch, but as a medicine; wine and meat must be most sparingly used; beds, chairs, and tables become ponderous luxuries, which can be only occasionally met with; but perhaps the worst privation of all is the want of a good house, wherein to seek some repose and rest from the intolerable heat of the sun. A small, low hut of clay and thatch is but too often the only place of rest during the heat of the day, after a night spent in the saddle or cart, and a long morning in prayer and instruction amongst the Christians. His clothing, too, is entirely changed, and consists of a white or yellow soutane, called an *angwy*, of native shape; a red sash; and a flowing muslin scarf, worn either over the shoulders, or around the head as a turban over the red cap made in the same shape as that of the penitents of the country; the feet are protected by wooden sandals or red slippers. This costume, worn with a long flowing beard, forms such an *ensemble* that the European is with difficulty recognised at first sight. Besides his change in food, habitation, and dress, the Indian missioner must also change his whole exterior, and never indulge in friendly, familiar conversation, except in private, when he may chance to meet a *confrère.* With the Hindoos, whether Christian disciples or servants, he must be amiable, kind, and very charitable, but must stand on the greatest reserve, and keep every one at the most formal distance. He must never think of eating with or in the presence of his congregation, and his disciples and servants must always stand respectfully in his presence.

The missioner's habitual daily life is to travel from village to village, to administer the Holy Sacraments to his people. At all those villages where he makes a casual or annual visit he is received with triumph by the assembled Christians, who come out to meet him with flags and native music,* and conduct him to the church or chapel, where, after the first usual prayers, he announces to the people the length of his stay, the order

* Native music is more noisy than melodious. The Hindoo cannot at all appreciate symphony or harmony. The more noise, the better the music. The instruments are, large and small drums and half-drums; a sort of screeching clarionet, blown with a reed, of loud and harsh notes, and small compass; also a combou, or very large S-shaped trumpet, which is a grand instrument for its purpose—the note is loud, clear, and ringing, braying, harsh, and brassy, or low, wailing, and plaintive, in turn. Those well skilled in the use of this instrument will continue an unbroken note or blended succession of notes for some minutes, without perceptible interruption. The total cessation of sound is prevented by blowing a very low, clear note with the last mouthful of air impelled into the instrument by the muscular action of the cheeks, whilst they inflate the lungs again through the nose.

of the prayers and duties for each day, and then gives them a fervent exhortation to profit by his presence, and approach the Sacraments worthily.

The following is the usual order of the day in a village visitation: At three in the afternoon the catechist assembles all those who are preparing for the Sacraments, and reads to them a Preparation for Confession, which explains the whole of the dogmatic belief, and also is mixed with fervent prayers to excite the necessary sentiments in the soul. The missioner then gives a public instruction, explaining the guilt of sin, and exhorting to contrition and amendment, and shows some striking pictures representing death, judgment, hell, and heaven, and the judgments of God upon sinners. These pictures often produce more effect upon their minds than the most fervent exhortations; and when they are well impressed with their meaning, he shows them the crucifix, and explains how our merciful Lord, by His death and suffering, has redeemed us all, and given us all grace, if we only choose to avail ourselves of His mercy. He speaks to them of the love of Christ, and of the infinite merits of His precious Blood, communicated to us in the Holy Sacraments. Then the Act of Contrition, and other beautiful Tamul prayers written by the ancient missioners, are recited. Then the confessions begin, and continue often till midnight, to be resumed again in the earliest morning before Mass. At sunrise in the morning the bell rings, to call all the people to Mass; and before it begins, the catechist reads the prayers and instructions for Holy Communion, which are followed by an instruction from the priest himself. During the Holy Sacrifice, the Acts of Faith, Hope, Charity, and Contrition are recited aloud by the catechist, to prepare the people for receiving the Body and Blood of our Blessed Lord in Holy Communion.

After Mass, there is another exhortation, to encourage all who have approached to the holy table to piety and perseverance. At nine a.m. the missioner takes his meagre breakfast, and says his own prayers and Office, and rests a little. In the afternoon he receives the visits of all those who may wish to speak to him or ask his advice; he settles all the disputes and difficulties which may be brought to his notice by the catechist or by the elders of the village. He also receives the visits and examines the motives and conduct of those who may wish to become Christians, and appoints and arranges due means for their instruction; or else on another day he baptises the children, examines the progress in catechism, and performs the marriages. Thus, in full employment, with little spare time, the week or ten days spent in the village pass by; and when the work is done, the Father goes on to another, to recommence the same labour. He leaves the village surrounded by his whole flock, whom he blesses at his departure, and goes on his way, accompanied by their prayers, half worn out with fatigue, but consoled by the real good done in the name and by the grace of Christ.

Thus the missioner, especially if his district be large, has never time to rest. His work is always intense, and very fatiguing; his food is indifferent; and, from the bad accommodation afforded by his small hut, his rest even at night is seldom sufficient to recruit his strength. It is no wonder, then, that so many have sunk under the fatigue, and rapidly added their names to the long list of those who have suffered and given their lives for love of Christ. And this sacrifice of valuable lives must continue until the means of the Mission are sufficient to supply better food to the Fathers, and until native priests can be formed and educated to live in the villages and reside amongst their flocks, as in Catholic countries.

The want of funds to support and educate priests has at times pressed so heavily on the Mission as in no small degree to paralyse its action; and therefore it has been necessary to appeal to the charity of Europe for assistance. Nor has that appeal been vain; and the funds so charitably given twelve years ago have been productive of immense fruits and developments in the Madura Mission. God, who knows and sees how each alms was given, and the good done by it, has doubtless, according to His own true promise, showered His blessings upon the charitable givers, and restored to them, even in this world, the hundredfold promised by the mouth of Christ Himself.*

The greater part of the missioners who have toiled in the new Mission of Madura, and raised it to its present

* The following mortuary list of the Jesuit Fathers and Brothers who have died since the reëstablishment of the Mission may not prove uninteresting; and as some who read this little book may find in it the name of a friend or acquaintance, it is worth inserting.

Names of Missioners who have died on the Madura Mission since its reëstablishment.

No.	Name.	Date of Death.	Time in Mission. Yrs.	Mo.	Dys.	Cause of Death.
1.	F. Fidèle Alex. Martin	May 30, 1840	2	8	3	
2.	F. Eduard de Bournet	June 15, 1840	0	6	0	
3.	F. Alex. de Sansardos	Feb. 3, 1843	1	8	0	Cholera.
4.	F. Victor Charignon	Feb. 21, 1843	0	8	0	Cholera.
5.	F. Pierre Faurie	July 3, 1843	0	10	0	
6.	F. L. Garnier de Falton	July 5, 1843	5	8	12	
7.	F. Pierre Deschamps	Oct. 17, 1843	0	1	17	Cholera.
8.	F. Louis du Ranquet	Nov. 8, 1843	6	0	0	Cholera.
9.	F. François Perrin	Nov. 12, 1843	0	2	12	
10.	F. Walter Clifford	May 2, 1844	3	0	0	
11.	F. Joseph Berlendis	Oct. 6, 1845	1	5	17	
12.	F. Victor Daugnac	May 7, 1846	1	8	0	
13.	F. Gabriel de St. Féréol	July 19, 1846	0	10	0	Cholera.
14.	F. Anthony O'Kenny	July 20, 1846	0	10	0	Cholera.

position of success, have been French. Some were Italians, and some few English. The Frenchman is undoubtedly the best missioner amongst the natives; for though often deficient in perseverance under difficulties in the ordinary concerns of life, he possesses a singular power of applying his whole energies to attaining the

No.	Name.	Date of Death.	Time in Mission.			Cause of Death.
			Yrs.	Mo.	Dys.	
15.	F. Désiré Audibert . .	July 22, 1846 .	2	3	0	Cholera.
16.	F. —. Barret	July 31, 1846 .	0	0	7	Cholera.
17.	Br. Almeida (Schol.)* .	July 20, 1847 .	0	2	24	
18.	Br. F. Alvares (Schol.)*	Jan. 23, 1849 .	1	3	0	Cholera.
19.	F. Charles Ponsdevier	Aug. 11, 1849 .	1	1	14	
20.	F. Dominique Sartorio	March 10, 1850	2	3	2	Cholera.
21.	F. Benjamin Cauneille	June 1, 1851 .	4	1	14	
22.	F. Pierre Brissaud . .	Oct. 30, 1851 .	9	1	0	
23.	F. Joseph, Sen. . . .	Nov. 20, 1852 .	3	6	11	
24.	F. Joseph Gury . . .	Aug. 4, 1853 .	14	6	0	
25.	F. Jean Galtier . . .	Aug. 25, 1853 .	5	9	0	Cholera.
26.	F. Prospère Bertrand .	March 23, 1854	9	11	0	
27.	F. Vincent Hugla . .	July 27, 1854 .	10	3	7	Cholera.
28.	F. Jean Combe . . .	Aug. 8, 1854 .	12	2	13	Cholera.
29.	F. Charles du Ranquet	Sept. 23, 1854 .	9	0	15	
30.	F. André Richard . .	Feb. 9, 1855 .	9	7	0	
31.	F. Jules Billas . . .	March 17, 1856	7	0	4	Cholera.
32.	F. Claude Compain	March 20, 1858	2	3	0	Cholera.
33.	F. Pierre Perrin . .	Aug. 19, 1858 .	18	1	0	
34.	F. Léopold Beausoit .	Dec. 3, 1858 .	5	3	0	
35.	F. Eusébe de Mont .	Dec. 25, 1858 .	1	10	6	Cholera.
36.	F. Ernest Rigot . . .	May 17, 1861 .	5	10	24	
37.	F. Antoine Rébitté . .	July 3, 1861 .	0	4	0	Cholera.
38.	F. Victor de Lorde . .	Oct. 20, 1861 .	3	8	13	
39.	F. Joseph Cunningham	Dec. 6, 1861 .	8	1	14	
40.	F. Victor du Ranquet .	March 2, 1862	13	8	0	Cholera.
41.	F. Jacques Wilmet .	Nov. 17, 1862 .	21	4	17	
42.	F. Jérôme Mazza . .	Dec. 31, 1862 .	13	8	0	
43.	F. Eugène Rossignol .	Jan. 25, 1863 .	2	4	0	Cholera.
44.	F. —. Vernière died near Aden, on his voyage to the Indies, of heat-apoplexy.					
45.	F. Marin Chevalier died in November 1863 in France, his health having obliged him to return. He had passed fifteen years on the Mission.					

* Novice.

immediate object in view. When he devotes himself to religion, his character loses its egotism, and acquires a motive for action which secures constant effort, and makes him ever ready to renew his sacrifice of self, and show his consideration for others both with natural politeness and supernatural charity. The Italian seldom leaves his own country, and remains too strongly wedded to his early ideas ever to be able entirely to cast them off like the Frenchman. He is therefore less supple and amiable, and less winning in his way of acting with the natives. The Englishman is the least fitted to succeed with the native, especially in a country where his race is dominant. However excellent and supernatural his motives and intentions may be, the great national fault of preference of what is English over every thing else constantly crops out; his presence is not only useful, but necessary in the great centres of European power in India, where none can succeed so well with his own countrymen; but his place is not amongst the timid Hindoos, toiling, with daily patience, to bring souls into the fold of Christ.

CHAPTER VII.

NOTICE ON THE LIVES OF F. MARTIN, F. LOUIS GARNIER, F. CLIFFORD, F. P. PERRIN, F. JACQUES WILMET.

FATHER ALEXANDER MARTIN.

FATHER ALEXANDER FIDELIS MARTIN was born at Nismes, 15th December 1798, of a pious family, in easy circumstances. After having finished his secular studies, at the age of twenty-one he entered the Society of Jesus, from a strong feeling of interior conviction that it was the will of God in his regard. This strong conviction, joined to his admiration for the excellences of religious life as a means to serve God with sincerity, supported him through his arduous career without any of those consolations and attractions of heartfelt affection for the religious state which make it such a happiness and blessing, even here below, to many. There are several, and those not the least efficient workers, who enter as labourers in the vineyard of Christ from the one strong conviction that it is "His will." Their whole life is a constant struggle between natural inclination and supernatural grace; their career is a daily cross patiently borne on the road to Calvary. Such a vocation is by no means less real or less solid than that of those who embrace religious life without hesitation or struggle. It is only doing for Christ, supported by faith and hope, what each one has to do for this world, if he would succeed in it.

F. Martin's theological studies were made at Rome

with good success; but he was remarkable for his firmness of character and steady regularity in all his duties. After his ordination he was sent into Portugal, whither the Jesuits had been recalled by Don Miguel. He was amongst the first of the Order to return to a kingdom from which the Jesuits had been so cruelly expelled by the unscrupulous Pombal. F. Martin and his companions were received with the greatest enthusiasm in the College of Coimbra, formerly so famous. Shortly after, however, war broke out between Don Miguel and Don Pedro, the ex-Emperor of Brazil, who pretended to the crown of Portugal in behalf of his daughter, Doña Maria. For the two years that the civil war lasted, F. Martin and his *confrères* were constantly employed in the hospitals attending the sick and wounded in the midst of cholera and typhus. Victory at length declared itself for Don Pedro; since which moment Portugal has hourly sunk in the scale of nations, and her national decline has been marked by her successive aggressions against the Catholic Church. One of the very first decrees of the victorious party was for the instant suppression of the Jesuits; and F. Martin, with his companions, were marched on foot, guarded and treated as felons, from Coimbra to Lisbon. There they were thrown into the prison of Fort St. Julian, where so many of their brethren some sixty years before had died and suffered under the cruel edicts of Pombal. The French Government having claimed them as subjects, they were, after a time, delivered from prison, and returned to France. For a year F. Martin lived in retirement and prayer, and seems then still more firmly than ever to have made those strong resolutions which form the soul to the more earnest service of God, and open the road to high sanctity. He resolved to attain to this sanctity, cost what it would. He strove for it, and not without success, though he had to struggle against more difficulties than most men, and to work painfully up the narrow way step by step. His was one of those characters which can only gain the crown of heaven by violence; and he never yielded, but fought to the end.

In 1836, when the Mission of Madura was restored to the Society, F. Martin was one of the four chosen for the important duty of reopening the Mission. And before the end of the following year, FF. Martin and Du Ranquet were duly installed in charge of the southern part of the Mission at Tinnevelly and Palamcottah.

This country is divided into two distinct districts, and inhabited by two very distinct races of people—the fishermen, or Paravas, along the coast from the Cape to Tuticorin, the lineal descendants of those converted by St. Francis Xavier; and the cultivators, or agricultural class. Amongst the fishermen great ignorance prevailed; for though there were still priests amongst them, their ignorance and indifference to their duties left the congregations entirely deprived of all the means of instruction, and exposed to vice, scandal, and superstition. Many of their priests were natives of Goa, and had consented to take charge of the churches in these distant parts of India merely as a means of enabling them to retire and live "at home at ease," after some years of absence spent in amassing money by every means in their power, and in the most sad forgetfulness of the holiness of their state.

At this time a native chief or prince, without any real legal authority, had immense influence over the whole caste of the Paravas. His will was law, and no one dared to oppose him. From his ungovernable character and intriguing spirit of falsehood, it was almost impossible to improve the morals or guide the religious ideas of those who were under his sway.

The other portion of the Mission consisted of the Christians who lived in the interior of the country, and who had been for years almost destitute of all religious assistance. It was chiefly amongst the heathens of this district that the great efforts of the much-boasted Protestant Mission of Tinnevelly were made, and for a time with considerable apparent success. One of their principal men was the German missionary Rhenius, who learnt the language perfectly, and was a man of unquestionable talent and energy of character. He used to say of himself, that if Luther had not made the Reformation, he would have tried it himself. Under his energetic and talented direction, the Protestant Mission of Tinnevelly was at its highest point of success.

This was the state of things when F. Martin and his companion arrived, to strive to build up again the kingdom of Christ and restore the former state of the Mission, so flourishing before our Fathers had been driven from it by the suppression of the Society in the last century. Full of confidence in God, they applied themselves earnestly to the task; and from that moment dates the gradual decay of the Protestant Mission, which is now rather a subject of distress than of congratulation to its supporters. Defections to Paganism also ceased to take place; several of those families which had relapsed were recovered again, and many Pagans were converted. The Christian congregations changed their whole appearance, and a new spirit was diffusing itself all around.

However, a trial—and a severe one—was in store for F. Martin. The chief of the Paravas on the coast, and some bad catechists in the interior, who had been the instruments of, and the gainers by, the money speculations of the Goanese priests, raised a violent opposition to the two Fathers, especially F. Martin. The great mass of the Christian population had been gained by the

Fathers, and remained true to them, in spite of the acts of violence, the schemes, and the vexatious and false lawsuits raised against them. Yet even here, as has so often happened in the history of more civilised countries, a turbulent minority determined to gain an end, and, indifferent as to what means they used, seemed likely to triumph for a time over their more numerous and timid brethren—timid because they were conscientious. At Tuticorin, F. Martin was literally driven out of the church; and the excitement became so violent that his superiors, in the hopes of allaying the storm, removed him from the place, and sent him as superior to the neighbouring district. Thus was an apparent peace established for a time only, to be disturbed by a more violent storm immediately after.

F. Martin found his new district of Marava in an almost hopeless state. The Goanese party, by raising that cry which often so instinctively and powerfully appeals to the Protestant English mind, had gained the unqualified support of the English magistrates. They exclaimed against the tyranny of Rome in sending out foreign priests to interfere with their vested interests; and immediately an order was passed by the magistrates, forbidding the Christian congregations to have any thing whatever to do with the French priests, even where the whole congregation was unanimous, and where their churches were built by and belonged to themselves. By these and several other regulations of a similar nature, the whole of the Catholic Christian population was completely discouraged; the memory of their old Fathers, who had converted their ancestors, made them long to be blessed with their presence; the fear of the regulations against them made them dread to declare too openly for them.

For seven months did F. Martin, with all the energy of his character, toil and labour amongst this frightened flock, encouraging them, preaching to them, bringing numbers back to the long-disused practices of religion. At length, over-fatigue and want of proper nourishment brought on dysentery, which, after some days, showed all the symptoms of cholera; and before any of his *confrères* could reach him to console him in his dying moments, he had breathed his last, at the village of Ideicatoor, in the midst of his Christians kneeling around him in earnest prayer. "Whether the Fathers come in time or not, I am in the hands of God—His holy will be done!—that is sufficient for me," were his last words.* F. Martin was of a singularly manly, energetic character, and had much to struggle with; his life was one of constant and severe mortification of himself. The Indians loved and revered him, both in life and after death; his tomb became a pilgrimage; and many Christians, and heathens too, testified to the favours they obtained.

Father Louis Garnier de Falton.

Father Louis Garnier was born in Franche Comté, the 12th February 1805, of an old French noble and military family. At the age of twenty, whilst making his studies at Paris, he felt himself called to the Society of Jesus. He offered himself at the novitiate of Mont Rouge, and was accepted, in 1825. He then went to Rome for his theological studies, and there made the acquaintance of the celebrated P. Ryllo. They became friends for life. When his studies were finished at Rome, F. Garnier returned to France, and gave himself heart

* F. Bertrand reached his hut a few hours after he had breathed his last, and with sorrowing heart laid in the grave this first life-offering of the restored Mission of Madura.

and soul to the laborious work of preaching missions with Father Sellier.

Soon after, being chosen as one of those who were to recommence the Jesuit Mission in South India, he started from Bordeaux, with his three companions,—FF. Bertrand, Martin, Du Ranquet. His first labours in India were at Pondicherry; but in 1838 he was put in charge of the large congregation at Trichinopoly, one of the largest in numbers in any part of India, and composed of all castes of natives, with a large half-caste population and a considerable European garrison. There, as in the other parts of the country, the native priests were entirely unfit for, and neglectful of, their high ecclesiastical duties, and sought for nothing but the means of making money. For many long years there had been neither confessions nor instructions, neither sermons nor even catechisms. The Catholic soldiers, especially, were bereft of all help, except being able to hear Mass in a miserable and ill-kept chapel, in the worst part of the native town, on Sundays. The state of religion in Trichinopoly, where it had once been so flourishing, told much in the neighbouring districts, and whole villages had ceased to be Christian, because there was no one to break to them the bread of life. Besides, and in consequence of this total want of instruction, the Christians were all split up into parties,—strife and quarrelling were rife amongst them, and the most mortal hatreds existed. The Christians in Trichinopoly and its neighbourhood amounted to about 10,000.

F. Garnier found himself alone in presence of the immense spiritual wants of this large population. He set to work with ardent zeal; and, in spite of the greatest opposition and difficulties from all quarters, he gradually succeeded in gaining ground; and Trichinopoly, instead of being one of the worst and most abandoned districts, became one of the best. The Indo-Portuguese priests were his most active and energetic enemies; but it would be impossible to enter into any detail of his crosses, his troubles, and his fatigues. His frank, soldierly bearing, his honourable and gentlemanly principles, soon gained him the good-will of the British officers, civil and military, with whom he came in contact. His energy, his justice, and his indefatigable industry in labouring for their welfare, gained him the respect and love, as well as the fear, of the Hindoos, amongst whom it may be said that these three qualities must always be found together,—they can neither respect nor love with any constancy where they do not fear. The great majority of the Christians gradually submitted to him in Trichinopoly, and he received the adhesion of all those to the north of the river Cauvery, as well as at Aöur and other places. At the same time he acquired possession of a large piece of ground in the cantonments, and there constructed a church, which is still one of the finest in the Mission, and is the Cathedral of the Bishop. F. Garnier also built an excellent house, in which he intended to establish a college; but as, later on, it was found that Trichinopoly was too unhealthy for such an establishment, the college was removed to Negapatam; and the house now serves as an excellent residence for the Bishop and his clergy. In one of his letters about this time he says: "I am always either in the combat or on the march: it is, then, impossible for me to give that care to the Christians which they need. I am constantly busy in reclaiming legally my rights, or refuting the numerous calumnies and falsehoods asserted against us. All this takes time; and I am unable to break the bread of life to the famished multitude of Christian hearts which press constantly around me. You have a number of Fathers in Europe who long to share in the cross and sufferings of our Blessed Lord. Oh, do, then, meet their wishes and grant their desires as soon as possible! Here they will have plenty to do and to suffer, and they will labour usefully for the glory of God."

Father Garnier, after some time, really succeeded in gathering up and consolidating the congregation of Trichinopoly. His magnificent new church was solemnly consecrated by the Bishop of Pondicherry; and, finding fresh help arrive from Europe, he made over the European military and half-caste congregation to the Hon. and Rev. F. Clifford, the first English Catholic priest who had ever been in that part of India, intrusted his large native congregation to others, and then went farther south to seek for new fields for his more experienced exertions, and for other Christians to reform and bring back to the open profession and practice of their religion.

The large and ancient native city of Madura was the fresh field of his labours—the city which gives its name to the whole Mission, and a title to the Vicar-Apostolic. There, too, he gathered the scattered and uninstructed Christians around, taught and disciplined them in the way their fathers had been taught to walk by the missioners of the old society, and there also he built a handsome church and a commodious house for the rest and retirement of the Fathers, who already filled or were hastening to the different posts around. At the same time, he gave the help of his talents and experience to the Fathers who were toiling in the districts of Marava and Dindigul, who were hard pressed on every side in their labours for their congregations.

By this time the labours and the success of F. Garnier were well known in Europe. He was looked upon as one of the most remarkable and successful of the missioners; his talent in conceiving, and rapidity in executing, what was really useful, struck all with admiration. Besides this, he had the peculiar and rare quality of making himself as much beloved as he was admired, as well both by the native Christians as by his European *confrères*. All these qualities seemed to indicate him as the best and most competent person to be named as Superior of the Mission, when F. Bertrand was obliged to resign and return to Europe from extreme ill health. And this return to Europe was only consented to by F. Bertrand, not because it gave him some hopes of health—for he was as ready as any other of his *confrères* to die at his post—but because the development of the Mission had rendered it absolutely necessary for some one well acquainted with all its wants and requirements to go to Europe. F. Garnier was therefore named Superior on the 15th August 1842, to the universal satisfaction and joy of all who knew him.

With his superiority began a new era for the Mission. He communicated to his brethren his own activity and energy, which has never been lost, and to which is mainly owing its present development. F. Garnier taught his *confrères* what might be attempted and what might be done by energetic zeal supported by a truly religious spirit. This feeling has become, as it were, traditional, and has been carefully fostered by the present Bishop, Mgr. Canoz.

If F. Garnier had done nothing else but infuse this spirit in his short superiority, it would have been a great deal; but, besides this, he continued his own personal labours more zealously than ever, and whilst directing the efforts of others, never spared his own.

This increase of labour and responsibility, joined to the indifference of the food which he allowed himself, gradually weakened his strength; and he was conscious of this, yet he would allow himself no rest.

Attacked at length with dysentery, he rallied for a time, and when the danger seemed past he was seized with cerebral congestion and erysipelas, and calmly expired at Madura, in the thirty-eighth year of his age, fortified with all the rites of the Church. He had spent eighteen years of his life in the Society and six on the Madura Mission. His loss was severely felt in the country by all his *confrères*, and by the Christians.

Some months later F. Garnier's body was carried to Trichinopoly, to be interred near the church which he had there built. Whilst he planned it, and toiled in the daily labour of carrying out its construction, with only native workmen to assist him, he encouraged himself with the thought that he was striving to raise a house worthy of the Holy Catholic Faith and the celebration of the Divine Mysteries; he little thought that he was also preparing the place of his own burial.

The Hon. and Rev. Walter Clifford.

This Father was brother to the late Lord Clifford, of Chudleigh, and was educated at the College of Stonyhurst. Feeling himself called to a religious life, he decided on joining the Society of Jesus, and his novitiate was made at Rome. Having completed it, he returned to England, was ordained priest, and for some years laboured most zealously on the English Mission, and distinguished himself by his indefatigable exertions.

Being obliged to spend some time in France, he met some of the Fathers who were about to start for the Madura Mission, and conversed much with them. Up to that time he had been opposed to Foreign Missions in general, saying that while there was so much to be done at home, and so few labourers, it was wrong to waste precious lives among heathen and savage nations. What he now saw and heard so completely changed his opinion, that, after making a retreat to ascertain what might be God's will in the matter, he felt called to offer himself for the Foreign Missions, and was at once accepted, and ordered to proceed to India. He did not even return to England to take leave of his friends and relations, but on the 23d February 1841 embarked with FF. Wilmet, De St. Sardos, and St. Cyr, on board the French ship *Ganges*, at Bordeaux.

The arrival of F. Clifford was a great benefit to the Mission, which was entirely in the hands of French priests, whose ignorance of English was a deplorable disadvantage in their intercourse with official persons, and whose true position had been much misunderstood. The presence of a clergyman of F. Clifford's rank tended much to prove that those with whom he was joined were really actuated by religious duty, and not by any sinister motives, in their struggles with the schismatics for the possession of the churches and property attached to the Mission. His zeal was of course smiled at as enthusiasm by the Protestants; but sincere enthusiasm commands respect even in those who do not share it, and it was soon seen that F. Clifford never hesitated to risk health or life for the interests of religion. Those who knew the difficulties which he had to encounter were astonished at the quantity of work he got through; for some months performing the whole of the duties at Trichinopoly, not only among the soldiers, but also among the native congregation, though his knowledge of Tamul could not be great in the short time he had been in the country. Two of his letters, which give an account of the deaths of two missioners mentioned in the preceding chapter, will give a better idea of his natural kindness of heart, and of the state of the Mission, than can be conveyed in any other way. The first is addressed to the Superior in France, and is dated from

"Trichinopoly, July 31st, 1843.

"P.C.

"Rev. Father,

"A few days ago I begged F. Perrin, who was detained here on account of the prevalence of cholera in the district, which made the labour too great for me alone, to inform you of our terrible loss, by sending you a copy of F. Tassis' letter, describing the last moments of our venerated Superior. O Rev. Father, I cannot tell you how deeply I felt the blow which has been sent us, and the more on account of the two other misfortunes which we had undergone this year, 1843! This third loss has pierced me to the heart. I did so love good F. Garnier! We suited each other so well! I know I have given way too much to grief; but, Rev. Father, what would you have? I was so much attached to him! May God forgive me; may He cease to afflict us, and turn aside from us His wrath!

"We had a solemn service here at Trichinopoly, for the repose of F. Garnier's soul, on the 10th July; and we were obliged to celebrate a second on the following day, because our soldiers wished to be present, and they had not been able to attend the first day. On both occasions the crowd was great, and their tears very touching. They entreat so earnestly to have his body here that F. Bertrand cannot refuse, and it must be brought hither as soon as possible. It is only fitting that this good Father should repose in the centre of the Mission, in the church he built, at the foot of the altar he had just finished ornamenting. There were more than five hundred Communions on the occasion of his death; our good Christians have set an example, which perhaps is seldom imitated in Europe, of the right way of lamenting a pastor and showing attachment to him,—that is, to offer for the repose of his soul the spotless Victim of our redemption. The funeral ceremony concluded, according to the custom of the country, by the catechist reading aloud the names of all the Fathers who have died in this Mission, and by prayers being again said for them.

"Alas! Rev. Father, I little thought then that a fresh name must soon be added to this melancholy list! The wound made in our hearts by F. Garnier's death was still bleeding when a new and scarcely less painful loss reopened it. Our Lord has been pleased to call to Himself our dear F. Peter Faurie, who died here, at Trichinopoly, on the 30th July, the eve of St. Ignatius, our holy Father. . . .

"In the evening our brave soldiers carried the body on their shoulders from the house to the church, amid a crowd of Christians, who, grieved to their inmost souls at seeing us thus fall one after another, sacrificing ourselves for them, filled the air with their cries and lamentations. It was left all night laid out in the midst of the Christians, who watched and prayed round the bier. In the morning I said Mass, and performed the obsequies according to our customs. Our soldiers and a crowd of Christians were present, showing their grief for this fresh loss by their tears and fervent prayers. It was a touching sight, Rev. Father; my very heart was moved by this unanimous cry of a whole people, sent up to the Father of mercy, beseeching Him to have pity on one who had wished to be the minister of His goodness towards them, if His adorable designs had allowed. This prayer of a people simple in their faith, and perhaps deserving by this very simplicity our Lord's praise, *I have not found such faith in Israel*, will surely have been heard and granted in heaven! May their cries one day resound in this holy temple, and thence mount to the throne of grace for my soul! I ask nothing better than to die in India, like the good Father whose loss we deplore, *in osculo Domini. Amen, amen.* . . .

"But whatever anguish we may feel, do not fear, Rev. Father, that the death of our beloved brothers and comrades will make us lose courage, or look backwards. Could we view thus wrongly an end so precious before the Lord? God preserve us from so far forgetting our honour as to feel the least hesitation. Let us be ready to die fighting for God. Let us not turn our glory into shame by shrinking from the cross, in which is our safety, our life, and our resurrection. I perhaps felt too natural and sensible a grief for the death of F. Garnier: that of F. Faurie, which I have just witnessed, far from having the same effect on me, fills me with the sweetest consolation. I shall never forget the filial piety with which he kissed the picture of the Blessed Virgin, his good mother, and the reliquary of our Father, St. Ignatius, nor the expression of faith, sweetness, and resignation with which his dying eyes were fixed on me, while I was recommending his soul to the sacred Heart of Jesus, which he so tenderly loved and invoked. May this death, then, encourage us all to go forward in the path which leads to our eternal country! *Festinemus ingredi in illam requiem.* . . .

"Rev. Father, pray for me that I may obtain final perseverance from the sacred Heart of Jesus, through the intercession of Mary, and of my holy patrons SS. Peter, Ignatius, Xavier, and Stanislaus; that I may, sinner as I am, die like this good Father, whom we lament, repeating from my heart: 'Command me to come to Thee, that with Thy saints I may praise Thee for ever and ever. Amen.' I recommend myself, therefore, to the Masses and prayers of your Reverence, and of all our Fathers and Brothers; and I beg you to accept the assurance of my profound respect, &c.

(Signed) "WALTER CLIFFORD, S.J."

The next letter is dated also from Trichinopoly, November 18, 1843, and is addressed to the Father Provincial.

"P. C.

"REV. FATHER,

"The Indian mails have several times brought you sad news, informing you of the sickness or death of some of our missioners. This one will renew your grief, by announcing the double loss we have just sustained, of two of our dear fellow-labourers. It has pleased the Lord to deprive us of FF. Louis du Ranquet and Francis Perrin, both carried off by cholera; the former at Strivegondom, near Palamcotty, on the 8th of November; the latter at Trichinopoly, on the 12th of this same month. I will say nothing of F. du Ranquet, because F. Wilmet, in whose arms he breathed his last, has undertaken this account; but I will tell you about F. Francis Perrin, to whom I gave the last consolations of religion. From the time of his arrival in India he was busy studying Tamul, and, as we mentioned in our last letters, was in good health. He had interrupted this employment for some days to make his annual retreat, and prepare for the Feast of St. Stanislaus Kostka, which we were to celebrate on the 13th of November. On Saturday the 11th he felt unwell, but thought it of no consequence, and said nothing. The following night he was seized with a sudden coldness, a symptom of cholera. As soon as ever I heard of his illness, I sent for an English physician, who attended him with the greatest care; but all was useless; the attack was too violent, and the disease became worse. The Father Superior himself was ill in bed, and I, therefore, gave F. Perrin the last

Sacraments. I need not tell you, who knew his piety, that he received them with the most perfect dispositions. During his retreat he had a feeling that God required him to make a complete sacrifice of himself, and he did so with his whole heart and with all his will. 'What a happy day for me!' he exclaimed, while we were praying, bathed in tears, round his bed of suffering,—'What a happy day for me! Do not weep; I am going to heaven!' I shall never forget what I felt when I saw him lift his hands and eyes to heaven with the most moving affection and the most perfect resignation to the will of God, when I suggested to him to unite his intentions in his last moments with those of our saints, and to enter into the sentiments they had at the hour of death: 'in particular,' I added, 'those of F. Claude Deschamps, your companion in your journey, who has already gone before you to glory.' How this thought touched him, and filled him with a sweet confidence that he would soon see his friend again in a better world! In these dispositions he calmly gave up his soul to God on the 12th November, about half-past eight o'clock in the evening.

"I think we might inscribe on the tomb of these two dear and fervent fellow-novices the beautiful words of the Church: *As in life they loved one another, so in death they are not divided.* Their souls will be re-united in heaven, as their bodies have been on earth. Let us hope that it may be so. Meanwhile, faithful to what fraternal charity requires of us, let us pray that this inestimable grace may soon be granted to them, and that they may enter without delay that happy dwelling in which suffering and death are feared no more.

"I must now recommend the whole Mission, and each of its members, to the Masses and prayers of the whole province. It is easy to understand how much we need this help, when we have death so continually before our eyes, amid the ravages of cholera, among persons who are in good health to-day, and whom we see lying on their biers a few hours after.

"I have the honour to be, &c.,

(Signed) "WALTER CLIFFORD, S.J."

F. Clifford never spared himself when he could hope to win souls to God. Being the first English priest who had been in the district, he soon acquired much influence with the Catholic soldiers of the European regiments stationed at Trichinopoly, and revived religious feelings in their hearts. For some time he had charge both of them and of the native congregation, with whom he succeeded wonderfully, considering that he never became very familiar with the Tamul language. But he was not long spared. In the fatal year 1843, he had a slight threatening of cholera, caught in attending the sick; but it passed off, and his health continued pretty good till May 1844, when, to the grief of the whole Mission, he was drowned in bathing. The account of his death sent by F. Canoz, now Vicar-Apostolic in Madura, to the Provincial in France, is worth inserting here. F. Canoz was on his way from Marava to Trichinopoly when he heard of the accident. He says:

"I learned on my road the sad news of the death of F. Clifford. This zealous Father cherished a hope of dying of cholera caught in attending the sick, which death was in his eyes the most desirable next to martyrdom. He never spared himself, and we often admired his generosity in flying to cholera patients. But God, whose judgments are impenetrable, had otherwise disposed: death awaited him in the water, which it is said he feared. On the 21st of May he set out from Trichinopoly to visit F. Bedin, and rested during the noon-day heat in a grove near the river Coliron, in which he thought he should like to bathe. He sent away his Hindoo attendants, and went into the water. As he did not know how to swim, he should have had the depth of the spot tried; but this precaution probably seemed needless to him. The poor Father stayed so long in the water that his attendants got uneasy, and went to the place where they had left him. They found nothing but his clothes on the river-bank; surprised and grieved, they searched the water long, but to no purpose. At length, when night came on, they hastened to tell F. Bedin, who was not above three miles off. He came instantly, bringing with him fishermen, who sought all night long, but with no better success. It was not till sunrise that one of them, who had cast his net in the deepest spot, found the body. They took it at once to Trichinopoly, where it was buried; all the soldiers whose chaplain F. Clifford had been were present, as were all the authorities of the place, thunderstruck at this tragical death: the soldiers begged leave to erect him a funeral monument at their own expense. F. Clifford had always been very zealous for the salvation of the soldiers, and this year had succeeded in bringing to confession several who had long neglected the Sacraments. On Sundays he usually preached with an earnestness which moved the most hardened. . . . .

"What more shall I tell you, Rev. Father, of this fresh blow that has been sent us? As for its victim, we may lessen your grief by assuring you that we have no uneasiness. F. Clifford had a most tender conscience, and he had been to confession at Trichinopoly the very day before this lamentable accident. Moreover, the Lord, who in His mercy was perhaps pleased to spare him the trial of a lingering death, which he had much feared, seemed to have given him a kind of presentiment of his approaching end. Three days before this misforfortune, a Christian had come to see him, and, contrary to his habit of never allowing long conversations, he spoke with him for nearly an hour and a half on spiritual subjects, and especially on the necessity of being always ready to die. Thus prepared by Providence, and animated with a most lively faith, there can be no doubt that he made at that moment generous acts, which might supply for the usual helps of religion. It is true that, viewing it with the eyes of faith, we should have preferred seeing him die of cholera caught among the sick, according to his own wish; but Providence has arranged otherwise, for the common good of all. If we may use the expression, he deserved such a death for the generosity with which he braved it; but it might perhaps have alarmed us more, as being a fresh proof of what the rest had to fear.

"It cannot be concealed that his death is in itself a great loss to the Mission. The name of F. Clifford was respected by the English: it was a support for us in case of need with the Government and the magistrates, on whom we depend. We counted on him for the college we intend to establish: he would have drawn pupils to it and directed the studies. God's holy will be done. If you can replace him by another English Father, you will do us a great service: an Englishman will always succeed better than we can with his own nation, whose manners, customs, and character he knows thoroughly."

F. Clifford himself had written to one of his sisters only three days before his death, consoling her for the loss of one of her sons, and he used these words, rendered remarkable by the event: "In the midst of life we are in death: who knows? perhaps the next post may bring you news that I too am no more!" And it was so.

Father Peter Perrin.

In reading the Lives of the Saints, or the accounts preserved of the less heroic holiness of those good men whose lives have left behind them "footprints on the sands of time," there is nothing more striking to the reflecting mind than the diversity of character which one meets, and the different qualities of usefulness, as well as different sorts of holiness, which each has severally attained. The reader has seen F. Martin toiling painfully, but unflinchingly, along the road to holiness, and by his firmness of character resisting evil in his own heart, and laboriously bringing others to good by his holy energy. The bold and chivalrous character of F. Garnier has something more attractive, as his strong wish to make the cause of religion triumph, aided by his unquestionable talents and courage, carry him over, rather than through, the great difficulties which surround him. Now another character comes on the scene —one of those holy and chosen souls, born, as it were, under the shadow of the sanctuary, whose life from earliest childhood was an unceasing yearning after all that was most agreeable to God, who entered on religious life from real love of its holiness, and who sought the will of God in all things, going so cheerfully along the road to heaven as to encourage others who were toiling along it, and make them love holiness for the very brightness it produced in the soul and conduct of so loving a model.

F. Peter Perrin was born at Lyons, in the year 1807. His parents were rich and very successful merchants. The name of his aunt, Mademoiselle Jaricot, is well known in the Catholic world as the humble and holy instrument made use of by Providence for the establishment of the Association for the Propagation of the Faith,* as well as of the Living Rosary.† Both these associations have spread through the whole Catholic world, and been the means of salvation, mercy, and grace to thousands. This holy woman was fondly attached to her nephew Peter, and devoted much of her time to his early education. To these early cares of his holy aunt young Perrin owed, in a great measure, his love of the Cross, his earnest piety, and the great purity of mind for which he was so conspicuous, even in his earliest days. His earnest love for the sacred humanity of our blessed Lord, and his affectionate devotion to the blessed Virgin Mother and to St. Joseph, who lived for so many years in constant and holy intercourse with Christ, naturally raised in his mind a desire to devote himself also to the service of God in an apostolic life. As soon as he had completed his first studies, he asked with earnestness to be admitted into the Society of Jesus. His father, who was tenderly attached to him, tried, by every fair and kind means, to retain him in the world, and succeeded in delaying his entrance into religion for

* The Propagation of the Faith was instituted at Lyons on the 2d of May 1822. Its object is, by alms and prayer, to assist those missioners who are labouring for the salvation of souls in infidel or schismatical countries. Pope Pius IX., as well as his two predecessors "of excellent memory," conferred many spiritual blessings on the society and its members. From its humble beginnings, it has now spread its influence all over the Christian world, and distributes alms exceeding five million francs a year in every clime and country.

† The Living Rosary consists of an association of pious people, who agree together to recite amongst them the whole of the fifteen mysteries each day. Each month the mysteries are distributed by ticket to the fifteen members comprising the *circle*. Thus the mysteries of the life of Christ are daily brought to mind, and, in presence of our dear Lord living and suffering, mercy and grace are asked and obtained.

four years. His great affection for his father made this trial most painful to him; but by earnest prayer to God and dutiful affection to his father he overcame all obstacles, and was at length admitted to the novitiate in 1828.

The early years of his religious life were spent in that exact observance of exterior rule and habitual fervour in prayer which always accompany the growth of superior sanctity. About 1840 he was ordained priest, and obtained the summit of his ambition by being allowed to number himself amongst a band of missioners, who were leaving France to recruit the Mission of Madura. The ship on board which he sailed put in at the island of Bourbon; and F. Perrin, ever intent on doing good, employed his leisure time in preparing a large number of children for their first Communion. His mission to the children of Bourbon is still remembered, and produced so great an effect that it gave the beginning to that movement and determination amongst the people of the island to have the Society amongst them, which resulted in the permanent establishment of the Jesuit Fathers at Bourbon, and the commencement of the Mission of Madagascar. So do the saints of God, as they pass along through this weary world, leave behind them the sweet savour of the Divine goodness which has inspired their holy works, and by their example awaken a love of goodness and holiness in the hearts of others.

After a few weeks more of sea voyage, F. Perrin and his companions landed in India, and soon reached the scene of their future labours, where some quickly succumbed to the climate. F. Perrin himself commenced a career of eighteen years' steady, cheerful toil in the service of his Divine Master. He soon showed himself to be one of the most fervent, zealous, and devoted of all his fellow-labourers. After five years spent in the north of the Mission, during which time he had diligently applied himself to the study of the Tamul language, he solicited employment in the district of Marava, which was the most uninviting for its soil and climate, and the most fatal to European constitutions.

The Marava district comprises the ancient kingdoms of Ramnad and Shevagunga. It is the least fertile portion of the peninsula. The roads are unusually bad, even for India. The water is also very bad. Scarce a year passes without a severe visitation from cholera; and the country is singularly destitute of those things which are most needed by a European constitution. Rice is very abundant and cheap, but there are neither fruits nor vegetables. The soil is light-coloured and sandy, and during the rains becomes so miry, that it is almost impossible for either men or animals to travel; whilst during the long dry season it becomes so dusty and bleached, under the burning rays of the sun, as almost to stifle and blind the traveller, causing a feeling of acute pain and fatigue in the eyes, and a difficulty in breathing from very want of air. We cannot be surprised, then, that this district has been little inhabited, and still less liked by the Europeans; and that it has been at all times as an open grave to the missioners who have gone to evangelise its inhabitants. Scarce a year has passed without its victim; and no wonder, when it is remembered that in no part of the Mission are the dwellings of the priests more wretched, or the churches poorer. The superiors had, by sad experience, long felt that to send a freshly arrived Father to this district was more than any constitution could support; and to send even those who were somewhat seasoned to the Indian climate was to devote them to a slow martyrdom, and shorten their career of usefulness: yet no district of the Mission was more earnestly sought and asked for by the Fathers, whether from a hope of a speedier crown in heaven, or to relieve their *confrères* from the sufferings entailed by the climate.

Having obtained his nomination to this district of Marava, F. Perrin devoted himself to his holy work with all his heart and soul, and by a special providence lived and laboured there for a longer time than any of his predecessors. After the serious and painful illnesses which he suffered there, he was often offered a change of district, but as often declined it. For thirteen years he toiled through the dust and heat, or laboured through the mud, of Marava, in search of souls. At first, with one other Father to assist him, he was able to meet the wants of the different congregations. Immediately after his death ten missioners were not too many to develop and consolidate all the good he had begun. The misconduct and neglect of the Goanese clergy had brought the name of a priest into contempt, and a Christian was looked on as an outcast. As he passed through the country on his missions of mercy, he drew all hearts to himself; and the children of the villages, even Pagans, ran to meet him as he approached, and followed him for a time, as he passed on with his cheerful word and kindly blessing. But all his time was not peaceful; many a storm of opposition and severe calumny was raised against him; but he overcame all by his patient, meek cheerfulness, and if at times he sowed in tears, towards the end of his career it was given to him to reap abundantly in joy. The excellent state of each congregation in his district, and the surprising knowledge of their religion shown by the children, was the astonishment of the Bishop and his brother missioners when they went to visit him.

His labours in Marava commenced in 1845, and he traversed the country in every direction, sowing on all sides the blessing of Heaven, catechising, instructing, preaching, and reforming abuses. The holiness and purity of his own soul gave him a particular power for inspiring a hatred of sin into the minds of his flock; his talent for catechising children was so singular, and his manner so interesting, that crowds of adults, both Christians and heathens, constantly gathered around the groups of children seated before him, to learn the first truths of religion. But still more instructive and striking was the wonderful devotion with which he performed the holy Stations of the Cross to large numbers of the assembled people. His fervent words figured to them the sufferings and sorrows of our Divine Lord, and the people prayed and wept, repented of their sins, and really amended their lives. The Catechism and the Stations of the Cross were his chief means in instructing and sanctifying his people; and as the knowledge of God and the love of Christ penetrated their hearts, their whole conduct and morals became so altered as to excite the wonder of the heathens, and cause many to commence their own conversion, by a sincere inquiry into the truths of religion.

Thus, in unceasing labour, years passed by, and he saw several of those whom he had instructed in youth grow up to manhood, edifying in their piety, and sincere in the practice of every Christian virtue. The face of the Christian villages was entirely changed, and order and strict religious discipline prevailed where neglect and disorder had triumphed before. Many a time Father Perrin was nearly worn out with fatigue; but he always rallied, and went on more fervently than ever. As he advanced in his career, his virtues became more brilliant than ever—the more he was known, the more he was beloved and revered. Some large villages at the east of his district had all along resisted his most earnest efforts for their conversion. Some time before his death, he went and dwelt amongst them. Many were converted, but the others became more obstinate than ever. Suddenly a violent conflagration broke out, and destroyed or unroofed almost the whole village. A heavy rain then fell, which soaked with wet all that had been spared by fire. The sufferings of the people caused cholera to break out mongst them, and hundreds were administered in their dying moments, and many buried by the hands of the holy missioner himself. His zeal and charity overcame the opposition of the most obstinate; the greater part made their submission. Some of the chiefs, however, held out; but, as if to show whose work it was, almost immediately after F. Perrin's death all the others submitted likewise to the Bishop, and put an end to the schism which had so long desolated the Mission.

At length the good Father's health gave way, but his cheerfulness never abandoned him; and his entire resignation to the will of God edified all around him. Towards the end of May 1858 he was seized with a violent attack of dysentery, and foretold to those around him that it was his last illness. Being ordered a change of air, he set out for the central city of Madura; but he was too much exhausted to travel, and at the large village of Shevagunga he became too ill to go any farther. Surrounded by his sorrowing Christians, he calmly and holily expired, and passed, we may hope, to a better world, on the 19th August 1858, aged fifty-one years, eighteen of which had been spent in the Indian Mission.

FATHER JAMES WILMET.

IN the obituary list of the previous chapter will be found the name of this kind and good old Father, who died full of years, and universally regretted. He was commonly known amongst his fellow-missioners as *Père la Joie;* and, in truth, he was always joyful, even in adverse circumstances; and when heavy affliction, in the shape of death or serious pecuniary embarrassment, distressed the community for a time, his serenity, peace, and confidence in God diffused consolation on all around him. F. Wilmet was born at Rulle, in Belgium, in the year 1793, and was ordained priest before he entered the Society. He spent many years as bursar, or father procurator, in several colleges of the Society in Europe, and was uniformly remarkable for his singular possession of what are called in the Catechism the fruits of the Holy Spirit—charity, joy, peace, patience, &c.

A strict and edifying observer of his Rule, he was likewise remarkable for his keen appreciation and enjoyment of such amusements and indulgences as are inseparable from college-life, and allowed at certain periods of the year. From his advanced age and his stamp of mind, being all his life buried in college accounts, he was thought the least likely person in the world to dream of a hard foreign mission. His vocation was a sudden one; for it happened that, on an occasion when letters telling of the deaths and hardships of the Madura Mission were one day being read in the refectory during dinner, he felt himself strongly called to devote himself to the service of his suffering brethren, and to try if his skill in accounts and economy could not put things on a better footing in Madura. His resolution once taken, he earnestly solicited to be allowed to join the next band of missioners who should go out to reinforce the labourers in Madura. At the same time, he began to lead a most mortified life, and to accustom himself beforehand to the exercise of those privations which would be inseparable from his future career. He had much difficulty in persuading his superiors to accede to his request, for his health was already much impaired by his long years of hard work at his desk. Moreover, he was forty-eight years of age,—too far advanced in life to be able to accustom himself to a severe life in so unhealthy a climate. His perseverance triumphed over every obstacle. His was evidently a call from God. When he at last obtained the permission he so earnestly sought, he was quite overjoyed, and made his adieux to the whole college of Brugelette with a cheerfulness which made a great impression on his brethren in religion and the numerous boys of the college, with whom he was a great favourite.

He sailed from Bordeaux on the 21st February 1841, with FF. St. Cyr, San Sardos, and Clifford. Of these, the first-named is now the only one living. After twenty-four years of constant labour, F. St. Cyr has now come to Europe a second time to seek that aid for his brethren which they so urgently need.

During the voyage F. Wilmot suffered severely from ill health; but his weary and painful illness, which at one time seemed serious, never made him for a moment regret the step he had taken. On his arrival in India, he applied himself with all the ardour of a young man to the difficult study of Tamul. His age made this too great a difficulty for him; and he was almost in despair about it, when he determined to seek by prayer from Heaven what he could not master by human industry. It is distinctly attested by those who were living with him, that, before Pentecost Sunday, the year after his arrival, he was unable to say any thing intelligibly in Tamul; and on that day and ever after he was, without further study, able to fulfil all the duties of a missioner—instruct, catechise, and administer the Sacraments; which he continued to do with much fruit till towards the end of his life, when his health entirely gave way. No one was more zealous, earnest, and indefatigable in all his duties than was kind old "Père la Joie," as he was named, with good reason, by his brethren. And it was this very quality which made his presence so valuable, and his arrival in the Mission a providence for all. Human nature will sometimes yield when obstacles seem insurmountable; and the hearts and minds even of those who serve God with earnestness, and accept all sorrows with perfect resignation, may, when too sorely tried, lose that elasticity and courage necessary for the continued vigour of action which can alone insure success. The numerous deaths; the depression of poverty, which scarcely allowed sufficient food; the scandals which existed in parts of the Mission which had long been deprived of priests; the constant opposition of the schismatic party, ever watchful to find an opportunity for aggression; joined to the system at first adopted, by which every disputed case of possession of Church property was decided against them by the English courts in the country,—all this had produced a feeling of depression amongst many of the Fathers which, while they consented to labour on, made them almost hopeless of ultimate success in the good work they had undertaken. It seemed the special mission of this excellent old Father to dispel the depression and disperse the sorrows by which his brethren were weighed down. His astonishing success in accomplishing this task would alone have made his presence invaluable in the Mission. His joyous ways and cheerful looks spread life and hope around him; and seeing one so old, comparatively, and so respected, hope against hope, and joyous under every adversity, made others hopeful and courageous too. The spirit infused by him has survived through many years of trial. His words of promise to his brethren, and of warning to the Christians, so often came true, both for weal and woe, that his opinion on matters of importance was earnestly sought and much valued.

For some few years F. Wilmet laboured with much success as a missioner amongst the Paravas on the coast of the fishery, where his zeal and warnings have left a lasting impression. He was then recalled to Trichinopoly, the head-quarters of the Mission, and put in charge of all the funds and accounts belonging to it. It was a great trial for him to be withdrawn from the active work of a missioner, which he loved; but he compensated himself for it by devoting all his spare time at Trichinopoly to instructing and confessing the native Christians. Thus years of usefulness went by, and old age and weakness came on; but the joy and peace of his soul seemed to increase as his bodily strength failed. At length, after a long and painful illness, during which his courage never failed, he quietly, and without any apparent agony or struggle, "fell asleep in the Lord," with his usual smile upon his lips. His name will ever be held in cheerful remembrance amongst the missioners of Madura.

The great secret of his joy was his strong and lively faith, by which he looked upon God as a loving Father, ever present, with power and will to help those who placed their trust in Him.

This holy love of God constantly led him to the foot of the altar in his spare time, to pour out his soul in earnest supplication for the welfare of the Mission. When his increasing infirmities rendered him in his old age unfit for active work, he asked what he was to do. "You must pray for every body," was the answer. "A la bonne heure," he said, with his usual gaiety; "je suis donc nommé le Père *Prieur* de la communauté."

CHAPTER VIII.

COLLEGE AND SEMINARY OF NEGAPATAM AND NATIVE CLERGY.

One of the first thoughts of the Jesuit Fathers, on the reëstablishment of the Mission of Madura, was to bring again into existence and efficiency a body of auxiliary clergy similar to that which had been formed in earlier days by the Fathers of the old Society, and had done such excellent service under their direction. The want of men and money, the oppositions raised on all sides, both by Protestants and Goanese schismatics, rendered it impossible to undertake any thing during the first years. At length, alarmed at the fearful mortality amongst the European Fathers, the necessity of providing some native priests became so incontestable, that it was resolved to make a beginning at every risk and sacrifice. In the year 1845 this beginning was made, and the College of Negapatam commenced its existence. In speaking of the idea of raising and educating a native clergy, it must not be understood that there were either hopes formed or expectations entertained of being able to form and organise in any given time an Indian clergy, intrinsically self-supporting, and capable of taking its governing members from its own body.

This idea is not only contrary to all precedent in ecclesiastical history, but, moreover, the Indian character is singularly unfitted for such responsibility, and incapable of the vigour and power necessary for fulfilling responsible positions. The only idea was at first, and is now, to raise a well-educated and virtuous subordinate clergy, who would be capable of meeting the wants of the native Christians under proper surveillance. Thus it has been the practice of the Church to act in the conversion of other nations of a stamp very superior to the Hindoo. Many of the first priests in Italy were of Jewish origin. Italy, in her turn, for over two hundred years, sent Bishops to Gaul, as Gaul did afterwards to Britain, and Britain in her turn to Germany. The Irish nation seems to be the only one which was, on her rapid conversion, almost immediately able to furnish her own clergy and support her own hierarchy, and, moreover, in a very few years to send forth zealous and learned missioners to other countries.

Only after long years of faith and practice of the holy Catholic religion can it be hoped that the Indian Christian Church will be able to suffice for its own wants, and become self-supporting; but, in the mean time, a most excellent and efficient auxiliary clergy can be easily formed, who, under European superintendence, will be most valuable, and even indispensable, in her steady development. The conviction of their utility, and the necessity even of their assistance in working out the detail of ecclesiastical labour and government, was so evident from the earliest times, that St. Francis Xavier himself established the College of St. Paul at Goa for this object. Later on, the native priests were found so useful, and many of them so zealous and holy, when properly guided and governed, that when the gradual increase of the old Missions required it, another college of the same sort was established at Ambalacate, near Cochin. In pursuance of the same idea, in presence of the same wants, but confiding solely in Divine Providence, the College of Negapatam was established in 1845.

The town of Negapatam is situated on one of those

numerous mouths by which the great river Cauvery, after fertilising the whole kingdom of Tanjore, empties itself into the Gulf of Bengal. In former times there was a college of the Society at Negapatam, but it was entirely destroyed by the Dutch when they expelled the Portuguese from the whole of the Coromandel Coast. The climate is far more healthy than in the interior. By sea there is access to Madras and the Island of Ceylon; by rail there is now also communication with Trichinopoly, and the railway will soon be extended to the other sea.

The schools were opened, in houses hired for the purpose, by Rev. FF. St. Cyr and Audibert; and for many months there was no possibility of giving them further assistance. After eighteen months, F. Audibert sank under the fatigue.

Soon after, a piece of ground was obtained from the Government at a heavy rent. On this were first raised some temporary buildings, in which the schools were carried on for some years. A number of high-caste native boys were regularly organised into classes in a separate part of the building; so that European, half-caste, and native boys were all under instruction in one establishment, and taught by the same professors. The college seemed to promise a solid success, and it became necessary to erect permanent buildings, capable of accommodating the schools and the Fathers. The total want of funds was most disheartening; but F. St. Cyr was determined to try, and, with the assistance of F. Strickland, found means to prepare materials and to dig foundations. On the Feast of the Exaltation of the Holy Cross, 14th September 1847, the first stone or brick was placed, with the solemn ceremonies and prayers of the Church. It was a family festival. After the rector had placed the first brick, each of the community and each boy—European and native, down to the very youngest—

advanced in their turn and laid the foundations of a college which has since become a handsome edifice, and contributed much to raise our holy religion in the estimation of the people of the country.

In this good work, however, as in all others which contribute to the glory of God, trials were not wanting.

The year 1846 opened with the happiest prospects to the college. More pupils were offered than could find room; but sixty-five were received, whose good conduct and diligence gave great hopes for their future career. This was interrupted by the breaking out of cholera, when three of the Fathers were carried off, and six of the scholars were attacked,—two of whom, a native boy and an Armenian, died. The latter was the hope of his family. The utmost terror now pervaded the school. The boys were immediately sent to their parents and relations; those who had none near were removed, under the care of F. Tassis, to Karical, and the alarm subsided; but the college was closed for three months. On its reopening, few pupils appeared; but this was fully expected after such a fearful interruption.

In the night of the 11th of September 1848, the temporary dwelling in which the college was carried on was set on fire by the schismatics, who had long been jealous of the strength it gained for the Catholic cause, and the attention it drew. All the inmates were asleep at the time; but happily no lives were lost, though a few minutes were enough to wrap in flames the whole slight building, which was roofed only with cocoa-nut leaves. Of course the first object was to save the pupils; and so rapid was the progress of the conflagration, that scarcely any thing else was rescued. All the furniture, with the library, which was well chosen and somewhat extensive,—in short, all they possessed, even to the greater part of their clothes,—were destroyed. This crime was, according to all human probability, committed by the schismatics; there were proofs quite sufficient to have brought it home to them legally, but it was not followed up actively, and no punishment was inflicted.

F. St. Cyr, the Superior, with characteristic energy, saw plainly that they must contrive to carry on the establishment with as little interruption as possible. He used for this purpose all the money he could in any way command, and trusted to Providence to enable him to pay such debts as were unavoidably incurred. There was a general feeling in its favour among the Protestants and Hindoos, as well as among the Catholics; and the works were pushed forward so energetically, that, thirteen days after the fire, Mass was celebrated in the new chapel, and five days later all the Fathers, and their pupils, were established in the new temporary building. The great expense of buying afresh so many articles indispensable for daily use entailed severe privations on the Fathers, who endeavoured, by denying themselves in every possible way, to spare the very limited funds of the Mission, and contrive to go on with the college. They did not leave off the erection of the permanent building, and were helped by subscriptions from Europe, small in amount, but so unexpected as to give them great encouragement. Subscriptions were also raised in the country by F. Strickland; and about Easter 1850 a portion of the house was habitable. Early in 1851 the Fathers, and the pupils of European origin, were established in it; while the Indian boys and their teachers remained in the temporary dwelling.

By constant, steady perseverance, and devoting every available rupee to its construction, the college was gradually finished so far as to excite the surprise and merit the warm praise of Sir Charles Trevellyan in his official minute, when, as Governor of Madras, he paid it a visit.

It is one of the largest European establishments for native education in India, and certainly by far the most successful; but up to the present time it has never received the least help or assistance from Government. Even the ground-rent has not been remitted.

The impossibility of carrying on such an establishment without funds is apparent; the difficulty of procuring them is great. The Government approves and praises, but gives no help. The idea of paying for his education has not yet entered practically into the mind of the native. And no wonder; for, though their number is much diminished, there still are many Protestant schools in the country, supported by ample funds from Europe and America, where money is regularly given to the children who attend, or to their parents.

Can Catholics remain indifferent while Protestants make such enormous efforts? There are at least 160,000 Catholics in the district of Madura, but almost all of them too poor to contribute any thing like sufficient for the support of the missioners, however inexpensively they may live. One-twentieth part of the sums spent annually by the Protestant Missions would suffice to maintain the Catholic one in affluence, to found schools and colleges, to educate young natives for the priesthood, or to train them as catechists, and thus would rapidly bring the heathens into the fold of Christ. There would be no difficulty in getting pupils, no need of bribes to persuade them to attend. The Catholic parents will of course prefer Catholic schools when they are accessible; and the high-caste Hindoos are more ready to send their sons to Catholic than to Protestant schools; first, because the mode of life of the Catholic missioner is such as wins their respect far more than that of the Protestant, with his wife, his comfortable establishment, and Paria servants; and, secondly, because in the Catholic schools every care is taken to avoid outraging those customs of caste which have no necessary connection with heathenism. Europeans will hardly believe how small a sum is sufficient for the support of a native pupil: 4*l*. a year will usually be enough; and is it possible that Catholics will refuse this? Any one giving as much as will produce 4*l*. annually will thus have one scholar permanently in the college—one who may become a native priest, and contribute to the salvation of thousands; or if not called to so high a vocation, or not fitted for it by his talents, he may become a catechist or a schoolmaster, thus preparing the way for the priest to follow and complete the good work of which he has sown the seeds; or, thirdly, he may qualify himself for an employment under Government, and by his position and influence may contribute powerfully to defend the Catholics, still so often unjustly oppressed and misrepresented by the heathens, the schismatics, and the Protestant preachers; or, at the very least, he may become a good father of a family, and by his education acquire influence in his village, by his example contribute to make others live as Christians should, and thus consolidate religion in India.

The results of the College of Negapatam have already been not inconsiderable as regards the number of priests added to the Mission, and most consoling as to their piety and excellent spirit. Five European priests have been there ordained; also five Indo-Portuguese, and six of pure Indian blood. Moreover, eight young men are at present within its walls, studying their theology; and about one hundred boys of the best castes in the country are now being educated there.

There seems to be no good work in the Mission which promises such important results as this seminary college. There certainly is none whose success and development the Bishop and Fathers have more at heart; for, on the one hand, the number of pupils must soon be doubled, to meet the growing wants of the Mission, and the increasing desire amongst the Christians to enjoy its advantages. On the other hand, the Mission is no longer able to spare from its small funds the sums necessary for the increase of the college. In Europe a sum of 50*l.* is necessary for the support of a boy in a college for one year. In India this sum would make a fund out of which a native boy could be supported for a succession of years, during all his studies, and prepared for the priesthood if called to it. The positive outlay for a boy is not much beyond 6*l.* a year, and money can be safely invested in India at 12*l.* per cent. The Indian boy needs neither hat, shoes, nor clothing, in a European sense. Two cloths of country material a year are sufficient for his covering; his bed is a mat; his drinking-cup, his hand dipped in the running stream; his plate, a plaintain-leaf, or other leaves pinned together with twigs or straws, and renewed every day; his knife and fork and spoon, such as Adam and Eve first used; his right hand (never the left) most scrupulously washed before and after meals.

There is another class of Christians which must not be forgotten in this place: the Eurasian, or half-caste,—that is, the descendants of European soldiers and others who have married native women or half-castes,—and whose children, in most instances, are Catholic; for though, unfortunately, not remarkable for the practice of religion, still the greater part of the mothers have been born and baptised Catholics, and adhere to their faith with wonderful, and even edifying, tenacity. In cantonments and stations where proper means of religious instruction are given, the women and children are quite as good and edifying as many Europeans of their class. In ordinary circumstances, they are good, faithful, and very patient wives, and make better helpmates than European women to the European soldier. From the utter want of Catholic schools suited to their station, many of the children were educated solely in regimental schools, or in Protestant establishments; and, strange to say, a large number of them, as soon as they were married, even to Protestant soldiers, returned to the faith in which they were baptised, and insisted also on having their children baptised and brought up as Catholics. A great many, of course, were lost to the Catholic faith; but several either never forgot the faith of their baptism, or returned to it by conversion in after life. Protestantism had no charms for them.

Boys of this race have the same requirements as European boys: their clothing and food must be such, at least, as poor lads in Europe would be glad to possess, and therefore they cannot be provided for so easily as native boys: 10*l.* a year is the lowest at which they can be supported. They are generally quick at learning, and docile, but easily forget what they have learned, and are too inert of character to come to much positive good without great care and trouble. Another, and perhaps, in some regards, a superior class of these boys, are hereditary descendants from Portuguese families; bear the best old names of the country of their forefathers; are kindly, patient, and intelligent; have an inborn attachment to their faith; but are very susceptible and unstable, and are very easily intoxicated by success. They make excellent accountants and copyists, are good musicians, and form the mass of clerks and servants employed by Europeans in the large towns and in many large cantonments in India. They are inclined to real piety when well instructed; and from amongst the upper class of their families many of the best Indo-European priests have come in all times for the last three centuries. Yet both these classes—which, however, intermarry a good deal—require more care and superintendence than the European of pure blood or the high-caste native boy, and, on the whole, do not give the same satisfactory results. Without increasing the present buildings of the college, and without augmenting the staff of professors already necessarily employed, a good number of these boys might be well brought up, so as to choose from amongst them a select few for the priesthood, and enable the others to provide respectably for their future career as Catholics, instead of swelling the ranks of nominal Protestantism, or living with disedification as nominal Catholics. Hitherto, from its poverty, the Mission has been unable to meet the wants of this class, and much and increasing detriment to religion has ensued.

Wants in Europe are great and many; but, soul for soul, and alms for alms, there is more good to be done by money just now in the present state of the Madura Mission, than in any other Mission of the Catholic Church.

This chapter may be aptly concluded by the following extract from a short notice on the Madura Mission circulated some months ago:

"We come, therefore, to beg all friends of education and of Catholic Missions to give us some assistance. Each month forty-eight Masses are said for benefactors, and they are also constantly prayed for both by the missioners and their flocks. The education of native clergy is of vital importance; the small sum of 50*l.* is sufficient to make a foundation for the education of one native priest. For all contributors of this sum one hundred Masses will be said, and they will participate in the prayers and good works of the whole Mission."

CHAPTER IX.

CHRISTIAN CONGREGATIONS IN THE MADURA MISSION.

THOSE who have thought and talked of Catholic missions in India, whether in a friendly or unfriendly spirit, have often asked, What has become of the many thousands of converts made by St. Francis Xavier?—were his converts merely nominal? and was his passage through India like a brilliant meteor, leaving scarce a trace behind, save the memory of the wonder he caused in his bright moment of existence? In answer, it may be confidently affirmed that the passage of St. Francis Xavier has left immense fruits still existing in India, though that country formed but a small portion of the vast field of the labours of this great apostle; moreover, during the following centuries, whilst the Indian Missions continued to be worked by his brethren in religion, Christianity steadily advanced, each succeeding century seeing an increase of numbers. There was, it is true, a certain fluctuation: at one time, a rapid and great increase, caused by the immense influence and labours of a Beschi, a De Nobili, or a De Brito; at another time, a momentary reaction, produced by persecution.

It must not be imagined that the Madura Mission is now of the same size as when first established and defined under this name by F. de Nobili. The vast district of India formerly bearing this name in ecclesiastical records is now divided into five vicariates, only one of which preserves its ancient name. It is the largest in size, and possesses the largest number of

Christians, and alone has been again restored to the care of the Jesuit Fathers. The vicariates of Madras, Coimbatore, Mysore, and Pondicherry each contain a number of Christians, under the charge of Vicars-Apostolic. In the five vicariates now comprised in the ancient Mission of Madura, the total number of Christians will amount to 355,000 souls. Of these vicariates, Madura is by far the most important, both for its general population and the number of its Christians. The Christians of Madura, continually increasing, number 160,000, to which must be added about 20,000 schismatics within the confines of the vicariate, which extends from Cape Comorin to the river Cauvery, reaching down to the sea on the east and west, and bounded by the ghauts on the west. The Christians are to be found in greater or lesser numbers in almost every town and village of the country, and belong to nearly every class and caste of society; but by far the larger portion belong to the class of cultivators. Their numbers are steadily on the increase every year, both by the conversions which are made and by the great excess of births over deaths in the Christian population. Already in some few places the Christians are in the majority. In some villages the population is wholly Christian. They have generally found means to build a chapel, in which is placed a crucifix, an altar, and some few statues. There is a catechist in charge in each of these village chapels, who says the prayers publicly in the chapel morning and evening at fixed hours, instructs the children, teaches Catechism to all who choose to attend, and on Sunday recites the regular prayers and devotions appointed by the priest of his district. To this constant practice of public prayer it may be attributed that the Christians of Madura, though isolated in many cases and surrounded by heathens, though sometimes unable to hear Mass more than a few times in the year, or to approach the Sacraments, are nevertheless faithful, pious, and fervent. Three or four times a year the priest visits each village; and it is only then that the people are able to make their confessions, to hear a sermon or exhortation, and to approach the Holy Communion. Their children, although baptised by the catechist, have to wait for months to be regularly christened by the priest. In earlier times, some unfortunately died without being baptised; but few have now that misfortune since the establishment of the Confraternity of the Holy Childhood in the mission, which was set on foot by F. St. Cyr. When the time for making the first Communion has arrived, it is difficult in these small villages to give solemnity to the occasion by any of those striking ceremonies which are so great an exterior help to devotion, and leave such an impression in after life. It is only in the few large congregations where there is a resident priest that this can be done. The sick and dying are, however, most to be pitied in these isolated villages, as it is impossible for the priest to be present every where, especially in the almost annual seasons of epidemic disease, with a district of many scores of miles in length and breadth. It is true that the Divine mercy seems to compensate the dying Christians for being deprived of the great help of the last Sacraments by abundant graces; for constant experience has proved that they almost all die in the very best dispositions. Yet nothing can replace the want of the Holy Viaticum and the last anointing in the desires and affections of the believing Christian at the hour of death. To receive Him in love and penitence who is so soon to be a Judge, to have the erring senses anointed and blessed with the holy sign of the cross, is a priceless grace.

When the Christians who inhabit the villages where

there is no priest wish to assist at Mass, or to approach the holy Sacraments more frequently than the missioner is able to come to his village, he must make a long journey on foot; and of late years the fervour of the people has so much increased, that in every place where Mass is regularly said on Sundays the affluence is immense—so great, that the churches cannot contain the flock, and the Father is obliged to preach to and teach his children in the open air, either under the burning sun or late at night. At some of the great festivals the congregation will amount to 20,000, of whom more than a third are often heathens. They are attracted, not only by curiosity, but by an indescribable feeling of reverence, which they openly express; and they join their Christian friends in all the exteriors of worship, and behave in the most becoming way. There is scarcely ever a ceremony of this sort which is not the cause, or at least the occasion, of conversion to some of the heathens who have assisted thereat. The heartfelt worship of the Hindoo Christians, expressed by their deep exterior reverence of demeanour, is most striking; they assist at Mass in a way which shows the earnestness of their belief in the presence of God; and during the whole time they are in the church or assist at a religious ceremony, they seem never to lose the spirit of recollection. What a lesson to some Christians of Europe, who would perhaps pass by the poor Indian with contempt, pity his supposed ignorance, or half suspect him of superstition for giving such exterior evidence of "the faith that is in him"! A few of the vast and beautiful churches of Europe, left so often vacant by the "enlightened infidelity" of the day, would be a blessing and a treasure to the Hindoo Christians—a blessing, if we can compare the material to the spiritual, surpassing in its wide dimensions all that is most beautiful in the vastness and symmetry of our noblest cathedrals, and capable of raising their souls by faith (when praying in them) as near to heaven as were the pious hearts of those who built them to the honour and glory of God in the bygone ages of faith. What would become of the remains of this holy faith in Europe, if there were nothing but mud chapels instead of our handsome village churches, and if the priest were able to visit each village only two or three times a year? In the day of judgment what a testimony will the Christians of India give against their more favoured brethren in Europe! There is, alas! perhaps more sin committed in one ordinary English town in a month, than in the whole Mission of Madura in a year. Such a thing as for a Christian to deliberately neglect or refuse to fulfil his Easter duties is unknown, and a very large proportion undertake long journeys, to be able to approach more frequently to the Sacrament. Blasphemy is never heard amongst them; the use of intoxicating liquors is abhorrent to the better castes; the days of fasting and abstinence are also most rigorously observed; and public decency is never outraged. If all this cannot be said with equal truth of the large cities and military cantonments, it must be owned with shame that contact with the European has caused much evil, and made the low-caste Christians who frequent the society of Europeans a very different sort of being from the simple villagers of the same caste in the country districts. It must at the same time be allowed, that if there is a great deal less vice in an Indian Christian population than in a European one of the same magnitude, still there are fewer examples of heroic virtue and self-sacrifice, to which the Asiatic character is imperfectly disposed. "Many, very many, of our Christians," said an experienced missioner, "will save their souls; but few will have a very high place in heaven." On one occasion a native Christian, the servant of an officer, had gravely committed himself. The master was very indignant, and the chaplain happened to call just whilst his ire was at the highest. The whole case was stated to the priest, and certainly there was but little to say to excuse the delinquent. Thereupon the colonel entered upon a violent tirade of the humbug of native conversions—professing Christianity, and practising none of its teachings. The chaplain quite agreed with him as far as the individual in question was concerned; and when, with considerable warmth and eloquence, the colonel had descanted on the subject for some time longer, the chaplain quietly rose, and wished his friend good morning, assuring him that the native Christians in the country villages really practised fervently what they believed, but admitted at the same time that, unfortunately, cantonment native Christians, from the examples set before them, *were often quite as bad as Europeans.* The colonel was less loud in his denunciations of native Christians ever after.

A few words about the churches, chapels, and oratories of the Mission will not here be out of place. In some few of the principal places of the Mission spacious and useful churches have been solidly built, though without much ornament—large enough to be really sufficient for local wants. Yet many other important and central stations have nothing but miserable sheds for churches, or hovels constructed of clay and reeds, and thatched with palm-leaves. In these places, meaner than the stable of Bethlehem, the Holy Sacrifice is offered, the Sacraments are administered, and the faithful assemble for their devotions. During the rainy season the calico canopy over the altar is insufficient to hinder the raindrops from falling upon it, and the pictures and statues become moulded with damp, and lose their shape and colour. The village chapels are, if possible, worse still, and are infested with bats, rats, serpents, scorpions, and other venomous animals.

Experience has shown that there is no material means possible by which religion would be more advanced than by good and handsome churches. Their construction raises the confidence and hopes of the Christian, and commands the respect of the heathen, who frequently comes to the Christian churches with his offerings and prayers to obtain some favour, especially when, as has often happened, he has learnt by experience that his prayers to the great God of the Christians are heard. And for how much can a respectable church—that is, a church or chapel that would command respect from this simple people—be built in the country parts? A small and decent village church could be raised for 40*l.* or 50*l.*; a handsome one, capable of containing 3000 persons, for 1000*l.*; and so in proportion. And if these sums seem very moderate, be it remembered they have hitherto been beyond the means of the missioner, however self-devoted and willing to accept hardships at the expense of his health. Moreover, with such small sums it would be impossible to do so much, were it not for the cheapness of material and the astonishing readiness of the Christians to give their work voluntarily, as a contribution to the building of their churches.

There are at present more than twenty villages where Christianity has been lately introduced, in which some sort of a chapel is needed to assemble the Christians and attract the Pagans. At Dindigul, which is the central station of a Christian district of 5000 souls, the only church is the dining-room of an old ruined English bungalow. The church there is to be built in honour of St. Joseph, to whom the Mission is dedicated. The royal city of Tanjore, with its 4000 Christians, has as yet no church; when built, it is to be dedicated to the Most Precious Blood. Ramnad, Pamjampatty, and other places, with 4000 or 5000 Christians, have only a miserable shed, open to all the winds, for a church; whilst other places, with from 8000 to 10,000 Christians, have still but unfinished churches, already suffering much damage for want of means to finish or keep them in good repair. And with such churches as have just now been described, no one will be astonished to hear that the dwellings of the priest, where he retires for rest after a long visit of administration, during which a tree or a small hut is his only shelter, is no better than the churches, and quite insufficient either to meet the wants or preserve the health of a European missioner. But the Fathers would never consent to the improvement of their own dwellings, till the far more urgent wants of the Mission have been supplied.

CHAPTER X.

LITERARY WORKS OF THE MISSIONERS.

THE whole of that part of India which lies south of the river Godavery bears the name of the country of Tamul, or Dravida. The language of this region is considered by the learned to be a primitive stock, from which are derived the Telinga, Maleialee, Cingalese, and Canarese dialects. Tamul is spoken at the present day by about 30,000,000 Hindoos. It is the universal language in the province of Madura.

Sharing the immobility which marks the character and the institutions of the Indian races, the Tamul language appears to have undergone no variation; the compositions of the most ancient authors whose writings have been preserved resemble exactly those which are produced at the present day. Moreover, in Tamul there are no local dialects, no *patois*, no vulgar corruptions. No trace of variation can be detected, unless it be found in a slight change of pronunciation in certain letters, or the more frequent use of particular words in one district than in another.

In common with all the nations of antiquity, the earliest compositions of this people were written in verse; the idea of works in prose is of very recent origin. The book of the *Védas*, and the *Ramaganam*, written in Sanscrit verse more than 1200 years before the Christian era, were translated at a very remote but unknown date into Tamul verse, and are universally diffused. The custom of writing in prose is modern, and does not appear to have become general till after the entry of Europeans into India.

The Jesuit missioners, from their first appearance in the country, in the time of St. Francis Xavier, devoted themselves to the study of the Indian languages, and especially of Tamul, the sole dialect of Madura, which was always esteemed their noblest Mission. F. Robert de Nobili, who was the real founder of the Mission, occupied ten years in acquiring a complete mastery of this language, and of the whole of its literature. It was especially its poetical treasures which engaged his attention. He spoke and wrote with equal elegance in verse and in prose, to the great admiration of the Indians. He was the author of numerous Tamul poems; but it was by his philosophical writings that his celebrity was chiefly acquired. Among other works, he composed a complete theological treatise on God and His attributes, and one on the soul and its spirituality. In a third work he refuted the Pagan arguments against the truths of religion. Numerous smaller books were composed by him for the use of the Christians. During the closing years of his long career, he may be said to have summed up all his various writings in his famous catechism, a work in four large volumes, which constitutes a complete *cursus* of theology.

These different compositions of the great missioners, who counted among his disciples so many thousand Brahmins, although they have now an antiquity of nearly three centuries, are still read, understood, and appreciated; the only reproach with which the native critics qualify their encomiums is this—that they are occasionally somewhat diffuse. But they do not take into account that F. de Nobili wrote for all classes, and had chiefly at heart to make the great truths of religion intelligible to all.

Other missioners followed the example of De Nobili, and enriched the language with many works of the highest merit. They were for the most part, as was natural, on religious subjects; and they have produced important fruits in the conversion of souls, and the diffusion of spiritual science. They will continue to do so in future years. In all of them the learned natives admire the profound knowledge which they display of the genius, character, and habits of their race.

In 1700 the celebrated F. Beschi arrived in India, where he was destined to acquire an immense reputation as a missioner, a philosopher, and a linguist. Constant Joseph Beschi was born about the year 1670; and having been admitted into the Society of Jesus, obtained the sanction of his superiors to devote his life to the conversion of the heathen. Madura had reason to bless the decree of Providence which gave to it such an apostle. If F. Beschi, in common with all his brethren, relied chiefly for success upon Divine aids, he was too wise to neglect human means. Having adopted, like his great predecessor, the costume and civil usages of the country, he applied himself with indefatigable ardour to the study of its languages. He became a master of Sanscrit and Telinga, and in Tamul seems to have surpassed even De Nobili. Not content with learning the spoken language, he acquired such a knowledge of all the best poets, that it was hardly an effort to him to discourse in Tamul verse. His grammar of the language is still the admiration of Oriental students. He published, also, a quadruple dictionary, in which he has earned the gratitude of Tamul poets, having dedicated one portion of it to their especial use, and furnished them with a copious selection of rhymes.

It would be tedious to enumerate even the titles of the many works which his fertile genius produced; but it is by his epic poem entitled *Tembavani*, read at this day with equal enthusiasm by Pagans and Christians, that his name is known with honour among all who speak the Tamul language. A brief account of this extraordinary work, for which we are indebted to a learned member of the Congregation of Foreign Missions, will not be out of place.

Oriental scholars are familiar with the celebrated epic poem *Ramaganam*, written in Sanscrit by Valmîki, many ages before the Christian era. It has been translated into all the languages of the country, and is read every where. Consecrated to the service of all the absurdities and abominations of Hindoo Paganism, it is admitted to be distinguished by rare poetical beauty, which has made it as dear to Indians as Virgil to Latins, or Homer to Greeks. F. Beschi resolved to oppose to the *Ramaganam* a poem which should dispute with it the admiration of learned Hindoos, while it should be occupied only with the truths of Christianity. The bold project was accomplished in the *Tembavani*, which has become a classical book for all ranks. The Mahommedans of Southern India speak of it with the same admiration as the Hindoos.

This poem, containing more than 14,000 verses, and therefore much longer than the great Virgilian epic, is said by our authority, confirmed by the oral report of one of the most accomplished Tamul scholars now living,* to be of such fascinating purity and elegance of style, such richness of expression and harmony of sound, that the reader is tempted to sing rather than to recite it. In the perfection of its rhythm and the variety of its measures, the latter being always adapted to the nature of the sentiments expressed, the author has courted and overcome all the difficulties with which Tamul poetry

* We refer to F. Louis Saint Cyr.

delights to contend. Sometimes there is a series of ten, fifteen, or twenty strophes (making forty, sixty, or eighty lines), each of which can be scanned in two, three, and even four different manners. "Only a poet of rare genius," we are assured, "and an absolute master of all the resources of the language, could effect such combinations."

The hero of this Tamul epic is the ever-blessed and glorious St. Joseph. The history of this saint being inseparably connected with that of the Immaculate Mother of God, the author has included in his vast plan all the historical events of the Old and New Testaments which symbolise or refer to these two privileged beings. The incarnation of the Son of God and the redemption of the world, in which so admirable a part was allotted to our Blessed Lady and St. Joseph, furnish the poet with themes higher than were ever sung in Tamul verse. It is from the Holy Scriptures that his subjects are derived. He has profited also by the revelations communicated by the Blessed Virgin to Maria d'Agréda. The poem is divided into thirty-six cantos, of which the first contains a magnificent description of the country of Judea, and the second of the city of Jerusalem. The birth of the saint, the wonders of his childhood, and his holy espousals, form the subjects of the three following cantos. The incomparable virtues of the Mother and foster-father of Jesus, the first sorrowful doubt of St. Joseph, and his subsequent joy, are said to be sung by the poet with a mastery of language and elevation of thought never surpassed.

All the mysteries of redemption, and of the life of Christ, find their place in this vast production, which was sent by the author to the native academy of Madura,*

* A learned body of natives then existing for the advancement of the literature of the country.

and earned for him from these Pagan judges the title of *Viramâmouniver*, or "the transcendent religious," by which name he is known at this day in India. It is worthy of observation, as F. Beschi remarked to these Indian academicians, that the title which they gave him was simply the translation of his own name, Constant, with the indication of his profession as a religious.

The reputation both of the poet and of his work has continued to increase to the present hour. Although a copy costs at least 30*s.*, a great number, executed either on paper or on palm-leaves, were constantly made; but by degrees various errors occurred in the transcription, which threatened to diminish its value. The original, in the handwriting of F. Beschi, which had come into the possession of Mr. Walter Elliot, a distinguished magistrate of the Madras Presidency, was generously lent by that gentleman to the missioners, by whom it was printed at Pondicherry, in 1851.

The writings of F. Rossi, one of the earlier Jesuit missionaries, known in the country by the name of *Sinna Savérien*, or "Little Xavier," which did much to maintain the faith of these people when deprived of their teachers, deserve particular mention. They include fifty-two sermons in honour of St. Joseph, to be read on the fifty-two Wednesdays of the year. They may be found in almost all the Indian churches, written on palm-leaves, and are read at evening prayers each week on that day.

The name of the great Christian patriarch, who is said to occupy the throne from which Lucifer was cast down, is now borne by a multitude of Indian Catholics, who have learned to cherish a filial confidence in his powerful protection. They have given it also to many of the new villages founded of late years, as—*Soussei-per-patnam*, city of Joseph; *Soussei-patti*, village of Joseph;

Soussei-abouram, town of Joseph. The agricultural orphanage of Dindigul, the seminary college of Negapatam, the orphan-school of Madura, and many other establishments, are under the patronage of the same venerable name.

Both F. Beschi and F. Rossi are known also by their controversial writings, to which the presence of Protestants and other heretics in India gave occasion. It was during the apostolate of the former that the Protestants began to arrive in the country. F. Beschi, with the superiority of his genius and the resources of his learning, exposed, in various works, the errors of these religionists. The most remarkable of his controversial treatises is the *Veda Velakkom*, or "Exposition of Religion," which is still regarded as the most effectual antidote to the poison of heresy; and is said by competent judges to be written with a force of logic and eloquence of style which the heretics can neither imitate nor gainsay.

As the number of Christians rapidly augmented under the teaching of such men as Beschi and his successors, the missioners could no longer suffice for the arduous task of instruction in a field which was constantly extending its limits. The events which already began to alarm thoughtful minds in Europe, and which were destined to assume a still graver character, presaged the coming day, when, at least for a time, the supply of missioners, upon which the progress of religion in India depended, would probably cease. It was under this apprehension, soon to be mournfully realised, that F. Rossi composed a series of works, to serve as guides to the natives when their teachers should be withdrawn, admirable in their method and arrangement, and inimitable in the intimate knowledge which they disclose of the character and mental habits of the Indian.

They are said to form a complete course of instruction in all his social and religious duties; and, having answered the special purpose for which they were designed, are still so highly appreciated in the happier times that have succeeded, that the most experienced missioners report in our own day, that "it would be difficult to find in any language a body of instruction more simple or more complete." It is these books which have powerfully contributed to preserve the faith among tens of thousands of Christians cruelly deprived of their apostolic guides, or abandoned to pastors too often mercenary and ignorant, and sometimes a scandal to their flocks and to the religion which they professed.

All these books, and others composed by missioners less illustrious, but not less devoted, were written upon palm-leaves with an iron style, and constitute a portion of the treasure of every church. Their value is so universally appreciated, that the Indian Christians, when seeking to obtain from God some particular grace, are in the habit of making a vow that, if their prayer be granted, they will transcribe one or more of them, and present it as a gift to some poor church or chapel.

It would perhaps be superfluous to speak of writings of another class—grammars, dictionaries, almanacs, and other scientific works—published by the Jesuit Fathers in earlier times, or of those which are now being produced both by them and by the excellent priests of the Congregation of Foreign Missions. Some of them have been admirably translated into English by Mr. Babington, of the Civil Service. The works which are constantly issuing from the press at Pondicherry find a rapid sale among the natives.

A translation of the New Testament has been published, and it is proposed to complete gradually the translation of the rest of the Bible. A Manual of Devotions to the Sacred Heart of Jesus, another of the Archconfraternity of the Sacred Heart of Mary, and a "Month of Mary," published in Tamul, have contributed to propagate devotions as dear to Catholics in India as in Europe. It is hardly necessary to add, that the Indians of Madura are able to read in their own language that incomparable book, the *Imitation of Christ*, reprinted, by the care of the Jesuit Fathers, in so great a multitude of dialects, and known as familiarly in the villages of Hindostan, the cities of China, and the plains of South America, as in the capitals of Europe.

It deserves to be specially noticed that the missioners have lately given their attention to the preparation of another class of books, designed to facilitate the study of Latin by young Indian students who propose to devote themselves to the service of the sanctuary.

There is only one obstacle to the still more rapid diffusion of those useful books, in the composition of which the Catholic missioners are as unrivalled as in the propagation of the faith; and it depends upon the Catholics of Europe to remove it. To them alone the missioners can appeal for aid. It is their zeal and charity which must supplement the insufficient resources of their brethren in India; and it may be said with truth, considering the uses to which their contributions are applied, and the results to which they invariably lead, that a given sum of money represents the application of the means of grace to a given number of souls. The salvation of the Indians depends not only upon the labours of their apostles, but upon the coöperation of all who belong to the household of faith. It is the will of God to employ human means and human agency, even in that combat between good and evil of which the issues depend solely upon His omnipotent grace; and it is one of the happiest fruits of this providential law, that it gives to the laity a share, not only in the magnificent ministry of the evangelist, but in the recompense which is to crown his toil.*

* "La gloire, le mérite, et la récompense de l'Apostolat n'appartiennent pas uniquement aux ouvriers évangéliques qui travaillent, combattent, et meurent dans la carrière. Les personnes pieuses et bienfaisantes, qui les aident de leurs prières et les soutiennent de leurs aumônes, y ont une grande part" (*Notice sur la Mission du Maduré*, par le P. Louis Saint Cyr, p. 23).

CHAPTER XI.

CATECHISMS AND PRAYERS USED IN THE MISSION.

St. Francis Xavier, in one of his letters, speaks of the great care which he took to instruct the Indians of his time in their Catechism and prayers, and to make them understand the Christian doctrine. In his exhortations also to his fellow-missioners, he constantly impressed them with the great importance of this duty of giving ample time and care to the teaching of the catechumens, and to the completion of the disciplining of their neophyte congregations after baptism. The successors of St. Francis never forget this early lesson; and in all times the solid instruction of the new Christians has been one of the heaviest portions of the missioner's labour.

F. de Nobili thought also that he could not devote his talents and power of expressing himself to better purpose than that of writing two catechisms, which are still in use and much admired: the first, a small one, which every child and adult catechumen was to learn by heart; and another, more detailed, developed for the use of the already instructed Christians, and the assistance of catechists.

Besides these two elementary works, which are still in constant use in the Mission, and in the hands of every catechist, there are other most useful books which are deserving of attention. F. Beschi, the most accomplished Tamul scholar who ever lived, wrote a most admirable work, in the very purest style, for the instruction and guidance of catechists in every single point of

Catholic doctrine. The Protestants, being unable to produce any thing superior to it, have reprinted this work, and largely used it for their own catechists, disfiguring it, however, with copious notes, full of abuse of many of the holiest doctrines it treats of. Besides this work, several other treatises have from time to time been written for their guidance. In fact, the catechist is not only valuable, but indispensable; and no wonder that in all times the Jesuit Fathers have taken much care in training and forming them. The greatest want felt by the Fathers on their return to Madura after sixty years of absence was that of catechists, and good material to form them.

A few words more must be said about this most useful and indispensable body of men. F. Martin, one of the most zealous of the missioners of the old Society, writing in the beginning of the eighteenth century, says: "Long experience has shown us that in ordinary circumstances a European can do but little to initiate the conversion of the Pagan; therefore we have endeavoured by every means in our power to form and train a number of young men, so as to make them good catechists." It is also related in the life of F. Bouchet, who distinguished himself about the same time in forming the Mission and building the still handsome church of Aöur, that, finding the work too great for the eleven catechists he already had in his district, he sold a silver chalice, so as to be able to support a twelfth with the proceeds. A catechist, in order to be really efficient, must be entirely devoted to the duties of his office, and must not have other work to occupy his time. They are for the most part married men, and, besides the small sum sanctioned by custom which they occasionally receive from the Christians, each one has an allowance of about six rupees (twelve shillings) a month from the Mission. When under good surveillance, their conduct is in general very edifying, and they seldom betray the confidence that is placed in them. Their position is one of honour and influence; and a catechist in every way fitted for his work is very much respected by his fellow-Christians. Public preaching in the streets is so entirely contrary to the genius and taste of the Hindoo, that it cannot be practised with any chance of success. The streets are the highways of the world, and those who are in them are on their worldly matters intent. When he prays, the Hindoo goes aside from the world to a place of prayer, or at least of retirement. Moreover, the received customs of the country, and their ideas of the exterior observance of morality, are so strict, that no stranger could ever enter a house to instruct a woman, nor could any but those of the lowest caste ever for a moment stop in public to mix with a listening crowd. A European missioner could never with any hope of success take the initiative with the heathen, and, by attacking his faith and proving its absurdity, bring him to a better mind. The first word of his foreign accent would awaken feelings of repulsion and susceptibility. The missioner would be at a disadvantage; and though he might by superior knowledge and power of reasoning silence or convince his opponent, he would not gain a single step towards his conversion.

The catechist, on the other hand, of Indian race and blood,—like to the people amongst whom he moves in all save his superior knowledge and piety,—passes through the country without exciting suspicion or awakening prejudice; he enters into conversation with the people on subjects of medicine, poetry, literature, or husbandry. A few words are quietly said about religion, sufficient to excite inquiry; some great truths are speculatively suggested; and the humble messenger of Christ, after some words of kindness and friendship to his new acquaintances, goes on his way with an inward prayer that his words may not have been in vain. The minds of those who have heard him, awakened to inquiry and aided by the silent workings of Divine grace, are better disposed to talk of serious matters and discuss questions of religion when next they meet. Thus the catechist gradually gains upon their hearts and convinces their understandings. He then more fully instructs them, and at length, when well prepared, brings them to the master of religion, to receive his blessing, and be admitted to the Sacraments in due time. Skilful and devoted catechists in this way, going industriously through the districts assigned to them, have always some converts under instruction, and at each great festival of the year bring them to the Father to be baptised. In many cases the administration of this Sacrament produces the most wonderful change, not only in the soul, which is of faith, but also in the body of the neophyte. Health has often been bestowed by its saving waters; and strength of body, as well as peace of mind, restored or granted where neither had existed before. The earnest and steadfast practical faith of those who have been duly received into the Church and baptised is one of the greatest consolations of the missioner, as it proves that the hand of God is with him, not only to guide him, but to confirm his work. The success of the catechist is often secured, and his labours abridged, by the casual presence of heathens who happen to assist at the celebration of the great Catholic festivals. Struck by the unwonted and deep reverential worship of the Christians around, they bow down to adore the, to them, "Unknown God," and rise up, if not believing, at least wishing to know more of the holy Christian religion.

The Pagan Hindoo, when he joins himself, from a sentiment of curiosity or of undefined reverence, to a congregation of Christians, listening to holy truths zealously preached, or intent upon profound adoration, is affected with very different feelings from those which he experiences when he sees a Protestant missionary in the ordinary dress of European life, and guarded by legal protection, stand up in the market-place or bazaar, and with irreverent gesture and vehement language impugn and vilify all that he has been taught from his earliest days to look upon as sacred. In a teacher of religion, a Hindoo expects to see great gravity and dignity of character and dress; nor are his perceptions sufficiently acute to recognise in the colour of a neck-tie the sole indication of the spiritual character of the wearer. Bishop Heber fully recognised that street-preaching was entirely useless in converting the Hindoo; and equally useless and detrimental is the aggressive method adopted by nearly all the various Protestant missionaries in India, of attacking and scoffing at idolatry before they have sown the seeds of Christianity in the heart. They have destroyed every vestige of religious feeling in the hearts of many; they have never made one sincerely humble, believing follower of the Cross of Christ. It was the advice and practice of FF. de Nobili, Beschi, and others, never to scoff at idolatry or turn it into ridicule until the mind of the neophyte was sufficiently imbued with Christianity to draw these conclusions for itself. By observing this wise practice, and thus showing a kindly personal consideration and a boundless charity for those amongst whom they labour, the Catholic missioner has gradually won for himself an amount of respect, even amongst the still heathen population, which immensely facilitates conversions. A large number of well-educated catechists would very much increase the annual conversions; for each active and intelligent catechist brings every year from fifty to a hundred persons (some of them heads of families) to the Father under whose direction he labours for baptism. The small sum of six or eight pounds sterling per annum is sufficient to maintain a catechist. Another proof how much good can be done in India for a very small sum of money in the present state of the Mission.

The old missioners, foreseeing the possible contingency of the Christians whom they were gathering to the faith being left without pastors, provided against this danger by so arranging the daily prayers which each catechumen was obliged to learn thoroughly before baptism, as to make the prayers themselves contain the principal dogmas of Christianity: by the daily recitation of these devotions, the acts of faith, hope, charity, and religion, essential for salvation, are infallibly known and practised. Some of these prayers are here translated; and the well-instructed Catholic will perceive how the worship of God by supreme adoration is clearly distinguished from the honour and reverence due to the ever-blessed Virgin and all the angels and saints who enjoy the beatific vision in heaven.

A.M.D.

PRAYERS IN USE AMONG THE HINDOO CHRISTIANS.

Prayer of the Holy Cross.

By the sign of the holy Cross, deliver us, O Lord, from all our enemies, in the name of the Father, and of the Son, and of the Holy Ghost.

[*While reciting this prayer, a cross is made on the forehead, mouth, and breast; afterwards, the ordinary sign of the Cross.*]

Pious Custom.

Ejaculatory Prayer on Awaking.

Jesus, Mary, Joseph, grant your protection, that my eyes in awaking may see no evil, and that my mind may indulge no bad thought.

Or, On Rising.

In the name of our Lord Jesus Christ, I arise. Grant, O Lord, that as I now leave the place of my rest, I may abandon every sin; and mercifully preserve me from again falling.

While Dressing.

Vouchsafe, O Lord, as I now clothe my body with these garments, to adorn my soul with Thy divine grace.

Act of Adoration.

Father, Son, and Holy Ghost, one God in Three Persons, I adore Thee with respect. I firmly believe all that Thou hast taught; I hope in Thee; I love Thee above all things; I thank Thee for all the benefits Thou hast granted to Thy poor servant, especially for having preserved my life till this day. I make a firm resolution to observe Thy commandments, without violating one. For this reason I offer Thee my thoughts, words, and actions, my soul and my body, so that all I possess may be devoted to Thy service. Accept all the good works I may perform, in union with the merits of our Lord Jesus Christ; and I desire to gain all the indulgences in my power, to satisfy for all my sins.

Save me, O Lord, by Thine infinite mercy!
Amen, sweet Jesus!

[*Then follows the Angelus, one Pater, one Gloria.*]

Morning Prayer.

[*On rising, the Christian ought to place himself on his knees, and, with joined hands, to recite with respect and fervour the following prayers, keeping his mind attentively fixed on God.*]

O Thou who art of Thyself, without beginning and without substance! Infinite Source of all good! present every where, by Thy intelligence, power, and action. Author and End of all things; who punishest the wicked by precipitating them into the flames of hell, and rewardest the just by bestowing on them the joys of heaven! Father, Son, and Holy Ghost, one God in Three Persons. O Lord, because Thou art the only true God, to Thee alone do I present the adoration that is Thy due.

[*While saying these words, adore God by prostrating the whole body with great humility. On rising, address the most pure and holy Mother of God by the following prayer:*]

Holy Mary, you are far above all other created intelligences. You surpass all the inhabitants of heaven by your innumerable perfections. You are the Queen of the world. You have been chosen the Mother of Jesus, true God and true man, without losing in the least your spotless virginity.

This is the reason of my offering you the tribute of respect and veneration which, by so many titles, is due unto you, far above all other saints.

[*While reciting these words the head should be humbly bowed, in token of great respect.*

Then, addressing the Holy Angel Guardian, and all the Angels and Saints, say the following prayer:]

All you glorious inhabitants of heaven, who rejoice in the clear vision of God; you who are the friends of the Lord, and can desire nothing but what is good; for your sakes, and through your prayers, our Lord each day confers new benefits on us. In acknowledgment of these, accept the respect and veneration I offer, in the spirit and intention of the Catholic Church.

[*While pronouncing these words make a profound inclination of the head, to show respect for the Saints; afterwards address Almighty God as follows:*]

O Lord my God, Thou hast created my body and soul out of nothing; and in order that this body and soul might live, Thou hast bestowed on me innumerable benefits.

Praise and thanksgiving be to Thee, O Lord!

O God of Majesty, who for my sake didst descend into this world, and, after becoming man, didst willingly endure most cruel torments, wert nailed to a cross, and didst die a most bitter and ignominious death!

Praise and thanksgiving be to Thee, O Lord!

By Baptism Thou didst mercifully apply to my soul the merits of Thy holy death.

Praise and thanksgiving be to Thee, O Lord!

After having received Baptism, I committed many sins; Thou didst mercifully pardon them by means of the Sacrament of Penance.

Praise and thanksgiving be to Thee, O Lord!

Thou didst invite me to partake of the divine food of the

Eucharist; Thou hast given me an Angel to guard me. For all these benefits, and an infinity of others which Thou dost not cease to lavish upon me, especially for having during the night past preserved my body and soul from all evil, I humbly offer Thee my thanksgiving, with all the gratitude of which I am capable.

Praise and thanksgiving to Thee, O Lord!

Prayer to offer oneself entirely to God.

Sovereign Master of the universe! it is Thou who hast vouchsafed to give me a body endowed with all its senses and natural faculties; a soul gifted with understanding, memory, and will. I offer all to Thee, in union with the merits of our Lord Jesus Christ, and those of all the Saints, as an agreeable offering to Thy divine Majesty. Since Thou hast given me all I possess, accept in return all the good works I shall perform from this moment till the end of my life.

To ask the assistance of God.

O Lord God, Thou whose power knows no limits, whose wisdom is immense and mercy infinite, I supplicate Thy Majesty, by the merits of Jesus Christ, to grant to Thy servant, to the Church, and to all mankind, the benefits of which we stand in need; but above all, to give me grace not to commit one sin this day, thereby walking in the path of virtue and good works.

[*Pater. Ave. Credo. Commandments of God and of the Church.*]

Act of Contrition.

My Lord and my God, continued Source of Mercy, because of Thine infinite perfections, I love Thee with my whole heart; and above all things, I am sorry for, and sincerely repent for, having offended Thy divine Majesty. This is the only motive of my sorrow. I resolve, with a firm will, never to commit these sins again; but as I can do nothing of myself, I beg most earnestly, that by the merits and sufferings of Thy Son Jesus Christ, and by the Blood He shed, Thou wilt grant me Thy grace, and vouchsafe me a place in Thy kingdom. I firmly believe all the truths the Church believes and teaches, because it is Thou who hast revealed them. Amen, sweet Jesus!

Resolution to practise Virtue.

My Lord and my God, I purpose to observe exactly the holy commandments Thou hast deigned to give me. For this end, I will resist all feelings of pride and anger, and every other bad passion that is within me; I will strive this day to do many good works, and to practise humility and purity in every word and action. But being of myself unable to keep these resolutions, I call upon thee, O most pure Mother of God, to pray for me to thy Divine Son. My good angel watch over me, and direct me in the path of virtue. Saint ——, whose name I bear, pray for me, that I may obtain the grace to serve God with fervour, as thou didst serve Him in this world, that so I may go with thee to see and praise Him for ever in heaven. Amen.

[*After these prayers, it would be well to recite the Rosary of Thirty-three Beads; afterwards, the Litany of the Holy Name, the Salve Regina, Acts of Faith, Hope, and Charity.*]

Night Prayers.

[*Begin with the Veni Sancte Spiritus, &c., and Emitte, &c.*]

Acts of Thanksgiving.

Lord, my God, Thou hast drawn me out of nothing, and made me man.

Praise and thanksgiving be to Thee, O Lord!

After choosing me from among Pagans, Thou continuest to pour Thy mercies on me.

Praise and thanksgiving be to Thee, O Lord!

The sins I have committed have deserved hell; being unable of myself to satisfy for them to Thy justice, Thy Divine Majesty deigned to become Man, to suffer and to atone for me.

Praise and thanksgiving be to Thee, O Lord!

Through the Holy Sacrament of Baptism Thou didst apply to me the merits of Thy sufferings.

Praise and thanksgiving be to Thee, O Lord!

After my Baptism I committed many sins; Thou hast forgiven them all by means of Confession, and instead of casting me into hell, Thou hast placed me in the way of salvation.

Praise and thanksgiving be to Thee, O Lord!

Besides the innumerable benefits Thou hast bestowed on me this day, Thou hast preserved me from all the evils the devil prepared for me.

Praise and thanksgiving be to Thee, O Lord!

Lord, grant me Thy grace, that I may discover all the sins I have committed this day, and that I may have a true sorrow for them.

[*Examen of conscience, following the order of the Commandments, of all sins committed since the last examen in thought, word, and deed. The Commandments of God and of the Church, and the Confiteor.*]

Act of Contrition.

Almighty Being, without beginning and without end, Lord my God, Thou art the Sovereign—I am but a vile slave; and nevertheless, without regard to Thy Divine Majesty, I have committed sins which have displeased Thee, I have meditated actions which are an abomination in Thy sight. Jesus, my Saviour, I have fastened Thee to the cross by my sins; often have I renewed the pain of Thy sacred Wounds. Lord, I, wretched sinner that I am, have caused Thee those indescribable torments Thou didst endure on the cross, and the cruel death Thou sufferedst. By my sins I have lost my soul; I have made it the slave of the devil; I have deserved to be cast into the flames of hell, to burn there for ever and ever, like a brand in a fire that will never be extinguished. Yet, Lord, I am less touched by the fear of hell or by the loss of heaven than by the contempt I have shown Thy Divine Majesty, infinite Source of all good. I regret, with the deepest sorrow, the sins by which I have offended Thee, the injuries I have conceived, and which have displeased Thee. These are the real causes of my sorrow, these my only affliction. I have committed these sins knowingly; deign to pardon me, O Lord. I resolve, firmly and determinately, never to commit them more; but as I can do nothing of myself, I beg most earnestly, that by the merits and sufferings of my Lord Jesus Christ, and by the blood He has shed, Thou wouldst forgive me my sins, and wouldst deign to give me a place in Thy kingdom. Holy Mother of God, pray for me to thy Divine Son. O Lord Jesus Christ, who takest away the sins of the world, be merciful to us!

[*Litany of the B. Virgin, Salve Regina, Acts of Faith, Hope, and Charity.*]

Act of Adoration before Retiring to Rest.

O Lord our God, Thou hast made the night that man might renew his strength by sleep. Praise be to Thee for this mercy! I thank Thee for all the blessings Thou hast granted me this day, and I beg pardon of Thy Divine Majesty for all the sins I have committed. I detest them, because they displease Thy infinite goodness, and oppose Thy greater glory. Watch over me during this night, and preserve me from sudden death, from evil dreams, and from all temptations of the devil. Ah, Jesus, grant that I may die in Thy grace and favour, that I may quit this world lovingly embracing Thy cross, and may go to enjoy Thee in Thy kingdom for all eternity. Amen, Jesus!

Meditation or Prayer on the Passion.

O Lord my God, who, to redeem the world, in Thine infinite mercy, didst become man, wert circumcised, and didst receive a kiss from an unworthy priest, Judas, Thy disciple; Thou wert bound and led like a lamb to be sacrificed; Thou didst endure contempt before Caiphas, Pilate, and Herod; Thou wert falsely accused, Thy face was buffeted, Thy body torn with stripes; Thou wert insulted, crowned with thorns, despoiled of Thy clothes, pierced with nails, and raised on a cross between two thieves; Thy thirst was assuaged with vinegar, Thy side pierced with a lance. O Lord, by Thy death, by Thy holy cross, and by all Thy torments, on which I am now meditating, grant that I may escape the fire of hell, and be merciful to me, as Thou wert merciful to the thief on Thy right hand, and to whom Thou gavest a place in Thy kingdom. Who livest and reignest, with the Father and the Holy Ghost, world without end. Amen, sweet Jesus!

O Lord Jesus Christ, when Thou wert on the cross Thou didst endure unheard-of torments, particularly at the moment when Thy holy soul separated from Thy body. By all these sufferings, deign to deliver my soul at the moment of death from the snares of my three enemies, the world, the flesh, and the devil, and to grant me eternal salvation. Jesus, our Saviour, who takest away the sins of the world, deign to efface mine!

[*This is repeated three times.*]

Vouchsafe to do good to those who injure us, and bring Pagans to the knowledge of the true faith.

God the Father, through our Lord Jesus Christ Thy Son, in whom Thou art always well pleased, and through the torments which He has endured for us, vouchsafe to forgive us our sins.

[*This is repeated three times. The Rosary is then said, and the Salve Regina.*]

Manner of Reciting the Rosary.

O Lord, Source of all good, although I am but an ungrateful and despicable slave, unworthy to appear in Thy Divine presence, confiding in Thy infinite mercy, I desire to recite this Rosary in honour of the ever-blessed Virgin Mary, Mother of God. Vouchsafe to grant me help, that I may recite it with fervour, and may banish all distractions.

[*Faith being the foundation of all virtues, recite first the Credo.*]

Holy Mary, daughter of the Father, although we are but miserable sinners, deign to obtain for us from Thy Divine Son the virtue of hope.

[*Ave Maria.*]

Holy Mary, in whom the Holy Ghost has placed all His delights, although but miserable sinners, deign to obtain for us from thy Divine Son the virtue of charity.

[*Ave Maria. Then say that prayer which Jesus Christ our Lord, true God and true Man, has taught us—Pater noster.*]

Joyful Mysteries.

First Decade.

What an inexpressible joy filled your heart, O holy Virgin, when the Angel saluted you with words of praise! After learning the object of his mission, you gave your consent with all possible humility, and God then became incarnate in your womb.

By the joy that filled your soul in the moment you became Mother of God, deign to pray for me, that, by love, He may reign in my heart.

Second Decade.

O holy Mother of God, being pressed by charity, you went to visit your cousin, St. Elizabeth, and your soul was filled with joy on seeing the graces that God had so mercifully bestowed on her.

By this joy I most humbly pray you to obtain for me true spiritual joy, despising the profane and perishable pleasures of earth.

Third Decade.

O Queen of Angels, my lips cannot express the joy that filled your soul when, without the least detriment to your virginity, you brought forth into the world Jesus the Redeemer.

Obtain for me, by this ineffable happiness, that your Divine Son may be born spiritually in my poor heart.

Fourth Decade.

Most pure Mother of God, forty days after the birth of your Divine Son you took Him to the Temple, in order to offer Him to the Eternal Father. How great was then your joy in hearing the praises that were bestowed on Him by so many holy persons who recognised His hidden greatness.

By this sweet joy I beg of you to ask of God that my poor heart may become a worthy temple for Him, by the sanctity and holiness of my life.

Fifth Decade.

Queen of the universe, having lost Jesus Christ, your beloved Son, you sought Him with great sorrow for the space of three days; but on finding Him in the Temple, surrounded by the doctors, your soul was inundated with joy.

By this your great joy, I beg of you to obtain of your Divine Son that my heart may be separated from Him by sin; and if ever I have the misfortune to lose Him, pray that I may find Him with promptitude, and that, finding Him, I may remain attached to Him for ever.

CHAPTER XII.

CONDITION OF WOMAN IN INDIA.

THE famous *Suniassi* (penitent) *Veichichta* has described in verses of great poetical beauty, originally composed in Sanscrit, and translated subsequently into the various dialects of the peninsula, the duties of the Indian woman. We present here some extracts from this poem, which has acquired the authority of a religious code, suppressing only such portions as European delicacy would be unable to tolerate. Nothing can indicate more clearly the notions and prejudices of the Hindoo races with respect to woman, nor the state of abjection to which she is reduced.

"Listen to me with attention, great king of Lilipa! I will teach you what should be the conduct of a woman devoted to her husband and her duties.

"There is no other god on earth for a woman but her husband. The most excellent of all good works which she can perform is to endeavour to please him, by displaying towards him the most perfect obedience. In this consists the sum of her devotion.

"Though her husband be misshapen, old, infirm, and of gross and repulsive manners; though he be violent, debauched, licentious, a drunkard, and a gambler; though he frequent places of evil fame, . . . neglect all his domestic affairs, and wander from place to place like a bad spirit; though he live without honour; though he be blind, deaf, dumb, or hump-backed; in a word, whatever his defects may be, whatever his baseness,

—a wife, penetrated with the conviction that he is her god, must be prodigal in her assiduities towards him, remain insensible to the blemishes of his character, and never be to him the occasion of any uneasiness.

"At every period of her life, woman's first duty is obedience. A daughter, it is to her father and mother that she owes submission; a wife, to her husband and his parents; a widow, to her sons. At no moment of her existence ought she to consider herself her own mistress.

"Let her give heed to perform with skill and diligence all the domestic labours of the house; be careful to restrain every movement of anger; never covet what belongs to others; engage in no quarrel; cease from no labour without the permission of her husband; and display an unvarying equanimity of conduct and temper.

"If she chance to see any object which she desires to possess, let her on no account venture to purchase it without the permission of her husband.

"Should her husband receive a visit from a stranger, she will retire with downcast eyes, and continue her occupation without paying the least attention to him. Her only thought must be for her husband, and she must never look on the face of any other man. By observing this line of conduct, she will merit the praises of all the world.

"Should any one offer her costly robes and precious jewels, ... by all the gods let her refuse so much as to hearken to his solicitations, and make haste to flee from his presence.

"When she sees her husband merry, she will laugh; when he is sorrowful, she will be sad; when he weeps, she will shed tears; when he speaks to her, she will be prompt to reply. By such conduct she will give proofs of her good disposition.

"She will carefully refrain from noticing that another man is young, or handsome, or of good figure, and, above all, from conversing with him. This demeanour will gain for her the reputation of a faithful wife.

"Exactly similar will be her conduct in contemplating the fairest images of the gods; she will regard them with disdain, as unworthy to be compared with her husband.

"The wife may never eat till the husband has finished his meal; if he fasts, she will do likewise; if he abstains from all nourishment, she will taste nothing; if he be in affliction, she will be cast down; if he be gay, she will share his mirth.

"Being less attached to her sons, her grandsons, or her jewels than to her husband, it will be her duty on the death of the latter to offer herself to be burned alive on the funeral pyre. Every one will applaud her virtue.

"She cannot serve with too much devotion her father-in law, her mother-in-law, and her husband; if therefore she should perceive that they are wasting all their substance in extravagance, it would be culpable on her part to complain; much more, to offer any opposition.

* * * * *

"To use the bath daily, to rub her body with saffron-water, to be clothed in clean garments, to paint her eyelids with antimony, to trace the red mark on her forehead, to comb and adjust her hair—these are occupations which will make her resemble Lackching (an Indian goddess).

* * * * *

"The wife must be careful to sweep the house daily, &c. &c. If her husband should go abroad in search of provisions, wood, flowers for the rite of Sandia (heathen sacrifice), or for any other purpose, she will watch for the moment of his return, haste to meet and conduct him into the house, present him a stool to sit upon, and set before him dishes prepared according to his taste.

"She will abstain from every kind of food for which her husband has no relish, and will refrain from anointing her head with oil when he does not first set her the example.

"If her husband, going on a journey, bid her accompany him, she will straightway follow. If he charge her to remain at home, she will not quit the house during his absence; nor until the day of his return will she make her ablutions, nor use oil for her head, nor clean her teeth, nor cut her nails; during the same period she will eat only once a day, will not sleep on a bed, nor wear new garments, nor adorn her forehead with the usual marks.

* * * * *

"A wife, during the absence of her husband, ought to neglect her dress; nor should she, under pretence of devotion to the gods, permit herself the exercise of pious practices.

"In presence of her husband, a wife ought not to look in this direction or that, but to keep her eyes fixed on him, in expectation of his orders. When he speaks, she must neither interrupt him nor address her speech to another; when he calls her, she must leave every thing and hasten to him. If he sings, she must be in an ecstasy of pleasure; if he dances, she must contemplate him with delight; if he discourses of science, she must listen with admiration. Finally, in his presence she must be always gay, and never exhibit any sign of heaviness or discontent.

"If her husband fall into a rage, breathe threats against her, utter the grossest injuries, and even beat her unjustly, she will only reply with words of sweetness, will try to seize his hands and kiss them, and will beg his forgiveness, rather than utter loud cries or run out of the house.

"There is for a wife no true happiness but that of which her husband is the source," &c. &c.

Such are the maxims, excluding many which will not bear translation, of the celebrated *Veichichta*, and such the position of the Hindoo wife and mother. In all communities, whose social life remains uninfluenced by Christian traditions, the lot of woman is the same. Every where she is abject and degraded, the slave rather than the companion of man. Only the Christian religion—teaching us to recognise in her, as in her husband, the image of God; declaring her to be redeemed, like him, by the Blood of the God-Man, and destined, like him, to eternal felicity—inspires the esteem, respect, and love which woman enjoys in every Christian land. The people of India are the inheritors of an ancient civilisation, possess laws which in general may be said to be good and equitable, and their manners often reflect by their simplicity the remote patriarchal ages. Yet they seem to regard woman only as a sort of domestic animal, a machine for the preparation of rice, a household slave. She is not regarded as a member of the family, of which all the male members are her masters; she cannot inherit the property of her relations, which passes to collateral heirs. She is not permitted to learn reading or writing, nor to apply herself to any kind of study. Arrived at a marriageable age, she is sold as a beast of burden to any one who will pay the stipulated price. No one ever thinks of asking her if she has any sympathy for the man who offers to purchase her as his wife. In her husband's house the most painful and the most disgusting tasks are reserved for her. It is her duty to prepare the food for her husband, her children, and her servants; but she must not partake of it till after they are satisfied. To pronounce the name of her husband would be an unpardonable offence, and she must salute him only with the titles of master, lord, and protector. If her children treat her with contempt and insult, or even with violence, she will rarely venture to complain. On a journey she must not presume to walk in the steps of her husband, nor to follow in the same line; and if there is any burden to carry, it is upon her shoulders that it will be laid. In widowhood, as we shall notice presently, her lot is still more sorrowful.

In presence of these facts, why should we be surprised at the moral and intellectual degradation of these unfortunate beings? Without joy in this life, they are without hope in the next. Upon none of our race has the malediction of sin fallen with a more intolerable burden. What words can paint the contrast between their lot and that of woman, surrounded with love and honour, in Christian lands?

There is only one remedy for these evils. Already it has begun to operate, and in those regions of India where the healing influence of the Catholic religion is felt, a marked amelioration in the lot of woman has followed. Instructed by the teaching of faith, men learn, as so many thousands have learned in China, where the condition of woman was still more base, that she has a common origin and a common destiny with themselves. Christian marriage, elevated in the Catholic Church to the dignity of a Sacrament, and therefore not dissoluble by divorce, bids the husband regard his wife as a part of himself, a companion whose weakness he must sustain, and who claims from him both love and esteem. The fourth commandment of the law admonishes his children that they owe to a mother the same affection, obedience, and respect as to a father. But do these Christian principles and this Catholic teaching suffice to uproot popular prejudices, and to restore to woman her true place in society? Assuredly not. It is further necessary that an education adapted to her sex and rank should elevate her in her own eyes, develop her intellectual faculties, and force the respect and homage which man never refuses to concede to wisdom and intelligence. In Europe we have founded, in order to accomplish this end, schools and other institutions for every class, where women and girls of all ranks are educated with indefatigable care, and cultivate assiduously those branches of knowledge proper to their mental and social grade, and tending to elevate them to an undisputed equality with the other sex. In countries more recently conquered to the faith, the same method has been applied, with proportionate results. In India, notwithstanding the peculiar difficulties and obstacles which our missioners encounter, they have dared to insist upon the education of women, and begin to reap the fruit of their patient labour. At first their efforts only provoked derision, violence, or calumny. A very small number of female children could be collected together, and the experiment was always liable to be interrupted by the caprice or prejudice of the parents. By degrees, and notably in certain districts, opposition diminished. As the children sensibly progressed, and began to display their newly acquired knowledge,—limited at first to reading, writing, arithmetic, and needlework,—hostility was conciliated, and public admiration excited. It is true that the novelty of their virtues was at least as persuasive as the wonders of their knowledge. It ceased to be a dishonour to a woman to be instructed, and then it became a title to esteem. At this day, and throughout the vast province of Madura, there is not perhaps a single centre of population in which our missioners could not open female schools, if they only possessed the material resources necessary for their support. It is in order to effect this object, and to show at the same time of what woman is capable under the influence of the Catholic religion, that the missioners in Mádura resolved to call to their aid the ladies of the Society of *Marie Réparatrice*, of whose labours we shall speak in the following chapter.

But there is another instrument, which the Catholic Church alone knows how to employ, for regenerating and ennobling the condition of woman; we refer to the religious life. The world has never witnessed a nobler spectacle than that which Europe presents in our own day, by the side of much that is full of sorrow and discouragement, in that vast collection of orders, societies, congregations, or associations, bound by various rules, in which thousands of religious women devote themselves to the acquisition of every spiritual excellence which grace can confer, and to the performance of every good work which charity can inspire. "Universally proscribed and dishonoured during the eighteenth century," says an illustrious writer, "in the nineteenth religious orders every where reappear."* On the burning plains of India, as in the snow-covered valleys of the Rocky Mountains, the heathen begins to profit by this revival; while Christians in the old world rejoice to see in this amazing multiplication of religious communities a proof that God is about to do some great thing for the glory of His Church, since He once more calls out of every land that consecrated army to whose peaceful victories humanity has owed in every age its best and most enduring benefits.

What these labourers will ultimately accomplish is perhaps reserved for our children to relate; meanwhile, it is impossible not to admire and respect these women,

* Montalembert.

who give us the example of so many and such lofty virtues. A certain number of European religious had already crossed the wide ocean to minister to the women of India. In witnessing their zeal and devotion, Paganism itself lifted up a cry of pleasure and astonishment; but the Hindoo was tempted at first to believe that a virtue so sublime was beyond his reach, and could be attained only by beings of another nature and a higher race. At length two or three institutions were formed for women of his own land, and then it was seen that Divine grace could perfect even in them the mystery of a religious vocation. The fervour, regularity, and perseverance of these new spouses of Jesus Christ surprised even Europeans, while the natives could find no explanation of the fact but by proclaiming it a miracle.

It was not, however, only with the object of forming holy religious that these institutions were created, but also that their inmates, instructed and refined by contact with the purest women of Europe, should labour, in their turn, for the education of their Indian sisters, become the spiritual mothers of orphans, and discharge all the other duties of charity to which their vocation impelled them. The number of these native religious is already sixty, and might be rapidly augmented, with immense fruit to themselves and to their Pagan kinsfolk and neighbours, if the resources of the Mission permitted such a development. In this, as in so many other fields of labour, it is the want of means which alone checks the progress of the missioners, and confines their operations within limits which, in a hundred directions, they are ready to overstep.

It remains to say a few words on the condition of Indian widows, and the measures which have been adopted to improve it.

We have seen that, according to the maxims of

Hindoo writers, the noblest action of which a widow is capable is to refuse to survive her husband. Of late years the influence of the English Government, which could not in any way connive at the crime of suicide and murder, has tended to abolish these detestable sacrifices. Women are no longer burned, together with their servants and jewels, on their husband's funeral pyre. But the lot of the widow, even when she consents to live, is sufficiently dismal. In the Mission of Madura, an immense progress has been made towards the amelioration of the position of Indian widows of the higher classes. Nothing, perhaps, affords more striking evidence of the growing power of religion in this country. At Trichinopoly a convent of widows has been established, under the direction of the religious of Marie Réparatrice, which contained in 1864 twenty inmates, animated by the best dispositions, and universally respected. Other widows seek admission, and poverty alone closes the door against them. Let the Catholics of Europe decide how long they shall seek an entrance in vain.

But this is not all which the influence of the Catholic religion has accomplished. The Christian populations of several considerable villages, all of high caste, have publicly announced their decision that widows, if they desire it, may marry again, without loss of consideration. Already more than a hundred widows have contracted a second marriage without incurring blame or disapproval. This example has become fruitful; and in the city of Madura eight marriages of this kind were solemnised on the same day.

The missioners entertain the expectation that this custom, so opposed to Hindoo usage and prejudice, will become general throughout the whole Mission. Thus, religion has destroyed one of the most deeply rooted prejudices of the Hindoo mind, and has accomplished a reform which neither the gold of the English nor the proposals of influential Hindoos had ever been able to effect. With respect to those widows who do not wish to enter upon a second marriage, it is the purpose of the missioners to establish, wherever circumstances permit, a sort of Third Order, whose members, constantly under the direction of European religious, will devote their lives, while continuing to reside with their families, to various works of zeal and charity.

CHAPTER XIII.

THE RELIGIOUS OF THE SOCIETY OF MARIE RÉPARATRICE.

For several years the Fathers of the Society of Jesus wished to obtain the services of a community of religious women, to share the burden of their toils in the province of Madura, and to extend to Indian mothers and daughters the blessings of that ministry by which European women, of all ranks and orders, have so long profited. It was necessary, in a country where the sex had fallen into contempt and abasement, to show what woman could become under the influence of Christianity. But only supernatural charity could accept so formidable a mission, and constrain weak and delicate women to forsake all in order to offer themselves as a sacrifice to God in so arduous a field. In addition to trials and difficulties common to all who profess the religious life, it was necessary in this case to brave the torrid climate of the interior, the insufficiency of food, the difficulty of an unknown language, and the almost total absence of the ordinary conveniences of life. But the Fathers resolved to appeal in the name of God to hearts capable of aspiring to such a mission, and they did not appeal in vain.

In 1859 F. Louis Saint Cyr, who has laboured for nearly a quarter of a century in the province of Madura, was in Europe on the affairs of his Mission. During his visit to Paris, he addressed himself to the Reverend Mother Marie de Jésus, Superior-General of the Society of Marie Réparatrice. He had found one able to comprehend his solicitude, and willing to share it. By her invitation, he explained to the assembled community the project which he had formed, and spoke to them of his Mission and its manifold wants in words so ardent and convincing, that all were inspired to seek the counsel of God, and devote themselves, with the Divine permission, to the new labour to which the fervent appeal of the missionary Fathers seemed to call them. Twelve volunteers presented themselves for the work, of whom seven were chosen and set apart; and towards the close of the same year they assembled at Marseilles, to commence the long journey which lay before them and the toils in which some were destined to lay down their lives.

The Superior-General accompanied her sisters to Marseilles, and it was by the sea-shore that they were to exchange their last greeting in this world. "Not a tear was shed," says one who witnessed the scene, "and God alone perceived the pangs of the sacrifice, since He alone was about to be *all in all* for these souls, anxious to labour only for heaven, and able to abandon with a smile on their lips, in order to open heaven to other souls, their country, and their home, and all the pure affections of family and religion." On the 27th of December 1859 they landed at Madras, and after a few days' repose set out by caravan for the city of Trichinopoly, which they reached in the evening of the 16th of January 1860.

So great was the curiosity and interest excited in the city—which contains a population of more than 100,000 souls—that the caravan could only advance slowly through the streets, the sisters reciting the *Te Deum* in thanksgiving for their safe arrival. The bells of the cathedral rang a peal of welcome, the square in front of the church was thronged with Christians, the doors were open, and the clergy stood on the steps to greet their arrival. It was with difficulty that they could make their way, after they had received benediction, through the crowd of rejoicing Indians to their temporary abode, which they found as mean and unfurnished as their love of poverty could desire, but which they were to inhabit for more than twelve months. As a specimen of the luxury which they found in this Indian dwelling, it may be mentioned that their bedding was composed of two blankets, of which one was offered as a gift by some English soldiers. The furniture consisted of seven chairs and a table, the latter afterwards converted into a humble altar; and when, some days after their arrival, they asked their medical attendant how it was that they were so little troubled by flies, the plague of India, he replied: "The explanation is very simple —there is nothing in your house."

The sisters had found only what they came to seek; and amid poverty and sickness, produced by heat and insufficient nutriment—even bread being generally too dear for their slender means—they commenced the labours to which they had devoted their lives. "Our house," they said once, in a letter to their Superior in Paris, "seems to us to resemble sufficiently the house at Nazareth;" and then they thought of it no more, or only to regret that it was so ill fitted to give shelter to the Indian widows and orphans whom they desired to succour and console.

A convent had been already founded at Trichinopoly for a small number of widows, whom it was now proposed to place under the direction of the European religious. From the period of its foundation scarcely a day had passed without new and urgent applications for admission. The reasons assigned by these widows for quitting their families and the world sufficiently indicated the misery of their unprotected state. If they had lamented only their solitude, the absence of sympathy and kindness, or even the danger of actual cruelty and violence, their case would have deserved prompt consideration; but it was of menaces against their honour, and of utter perdition, that these unhappy women had to tell. Yet the resources of the Mission were too inconsiderable to admit of any increase to the number already sheltered in the convent. In vain Christian widows, including some of the ages of fourteen and fifteen, implored a refuge within its walls. One of them, to whom it was promised that she should be received at a later period, abandoned herself to inconsolable grief, and spent night and day in tears. They were of different castes, but were willing to forget this bar, in order to dwell together in peace and retirement. "If we could receive them," wrote one of the sisters from Trichinopoly, "tomorrow we might have them of all ages, but we are compelled to refuse them for want of means,—exposed to evil treatment, and even to the loss of their souls. If dangers abound even in Catholic lands, what must it be in idolatrous countries? Yet it was our sad duty to refuse an asylum to these unhappy young women. So little would suffice! Some poor dwelling, in which they might labour and pray, would secure their happiness. Those already admitted condemn themselves—in order to contribute to their maintenance—to the labour of husking rice, so painful to a woman; and yet, though exhausted with fatigue, can hardly earn enough for their bare support."

It is to be observed, moreover, that up to this date the idea of the religious life for women was new in this part of India. It was only by incessant care and perseverance that the first subjects could be formed to an existence so opposed to their habits and natural character. Nor could they prudently be left to themselves, even when the notion of consecrating themselves to God had been fully embraced. For this reason it was resolved to place them under the direction of the European religious, whose Superior wisely suggested, in reply to the injunction of the Bishop, Mgr. Canoz, that the proposal to that effect should proceed from the native religious. In order the more readily to elicit from them such a proposition, it would have been expedient that they should quit their convent to share that of the Sisters of Marie Réparatrice; but this was rendered impossible by the scantiness of the accommodation of which the latter could dispose. It was decided, therefore, to invite them to spend the greater part of each day at the new convent, in order to acquire skill in works to which they had been hitherto strangers, and of which the difficulty seemed to them at first insurmountable. The use of the needle was hardly known to them; and the habits of Indian women, especially of certain castes, are so indolent and apathetic, so completely intolerant of any kind of voluntary toil, that it was only by the formation of a new character that they could be induced to accept this burden. They were taught, therefore, to understand the expiation of sin by labour, and to appreciate by the light of faith the holiness of the unwonted occupations prescribed to them.

The orphans also—of whom they had the exclusive charge before the arrival of the European community—accompanied them daily to their new tasks. The latter were instructed in various kinds of needlework, and profited by the fresher air which they breathed in the convent enclosure, the stifling atmosphere of their own miserable dwelling having proved fatal to nine of its inmates during the previous year. The number of these orphans gradually increased; but it was long before they could be lodged in a more suitable manner; and it was necessary to accept meanwhile, in a spirit of patience and resignation, the sufferings and embarrassments for which there was no other remedy.

By the following year, 1861—the sisters having now acquired an adequate knowledge of the Tamul language—it became possible to undertake other duties. The Christian children of the city of Trichinopoly, hitherto imperfectly instructed, were to find mothers and guardians in the daughters of Marie Réparatrice. Many had still to be prepared for their first Communion, and this was the task to which their new teachers eagerly devoted themselves. As they had no building of any kind at their disposition, it was in the open air that the classes were grouped, and "the whole neighbourhood," as one of the sisters writes, "resounded with their voices." From time to time their progress was tested by a catechist, until the day arrived when the Fathers of the Mission should themselves decide upon their fitness to approach the Holy Sacrament.

Twice a week two of the community proceeded to the military camp, to give the same instructions to the English children; but these labours did not satisfy their zeal. In so large a city there were many sick and suffering, and to these also they wished to devote themselves. "Find us," they wrote to their sisters in Europe, "charitable persons willing to found a hospital at Trichinopoly; in addition to the immediate benefits which the sick would derive from it, it would enable us to receive a larger number of widows, many of whom are deterred from coming to us by the painful and laborious duty of husking rice." Far from being discouraged by the necessity of new toils, it was only the difficulty of carrying their various projects into execution which gave uneasiness to the community of Marie Réparatrice.

In the beginning of October 1861 a reinforcement of six religious arrived in India; of whom one was doubly welcome on account of her knowledge of medicine: and at the same time the means of founding a hospital were supplied by a French lady, Madame de Noujon; who wished by this act to preserve the memory of a daughter of whom she had been deprived by death. Fifteen patients were immediately received; but it was necessary, even in a hospital, to distribute the accommodation with reference to the distinction of castes—an inconvenience which added sensibly to the cost of the first arrangements. A beginning was made, because the need was urgent, but it was made under every imaginable disadvantage; furniture, food, medicines,—every thing was wanting; and it was only from the bounty of Providence that they could be expected.

Meanwhile, even at this early date, not one of the sisters had escaped an attack of fever; and one was ordered to return to Europe, as the only chance of restoring her health. Insufficient nourishment, added to the ravages of such a climate, was too heavy a trial for these delicate women. "Activity diminishes," writes one of their number, "strength declines, but joy remains; nothing can disturb it. Poverty is our habitual companion, and during the past six months we have been without a farthing to spare. In India the missioners are extremely poor, the inhabitants burdened by heavy taxes, and our Christians generally without means. We must therefore receive every thing, or at least expect every thing, from Europe. Our personal destitution does not affect us, since we confide wholly in Divine Providence; but we are concerned at the failure of our first efforts to obtain the buildings necessary for our works, and an abode more worthy of Jesus. How much good would flow from a church in which the ceremonies of our holy religion could be duly solemnised!" "Send us linen," writes another, "for we have used all our own to repair what is used in the churches; and we can obtain none here, even if we had money to buy it. It is especially for a supply of linen for the vestments and altars that I appeal to your charity. Moreover, for the use of fifteen or sixteen religious, we have only four pairs of scissors; and when another pair is urgently wanted, the Indian women say to us, 'You have *kasti*—sorrow.'"

But the trials of every kind which beset them at the outset of their career, and which they were still to suffer with more or less intensity in succeeding years, were only a welcome augury of future success. It was thus that they wished to begin their Mission. Some were to sink under the burden, but this also was expected. After several months of serious and increasing illness, the Superior of the Trichinopoly convent—who we learn with satisfaction was an English lady, the rest of the community, with a single exception, being French—was ordered by the doctors to quit India. Attended by another sister, whose health was equally compromised, she reached Marseilles on the 15th of March 1862. "Thanks be to God," wrote the sisters from India to the Superior-General in Paris, "that you have recalled our dear Mother Superior; at least with you she will receive the care which she needs; while she remained with us it was our grief to see her want the simplest necessaries, for as a rule we cannot provide for our sick even so much as this."

In the absence of the Superior—who returned to India in the following year with a fresh company of labourers—there was no interruption to the progress of their good works. During the year 1862 a new building was erected within the convent enclosure; which furnished four large rooms—two for the use of the orphans, and two for children of the city residing with their families. "It is much to be regretted," wrote the Bishop at this time to the Superior-General in Paris, "that resources are wanting to build within the same enclosure a convent for the Indian religious, who suffer greatly, as well as the orphans lodged with them, in their present abode, from want of space and fresh air." This charitable aid was to receive its fulfilment at a later period.

Let us return for a moment to the hospital, of which we have recorded the humble beginning. "This hospital," says one of the religious, in an account of its development during the year 1862, "is truly a noble work of charity, and will be the field of a rich harvest for heaven. It is an asylum which will save many a soul from dying without the knowledge of God. In his hour of suffering the Indian consents to be taken to the hospital; by degrees he begins to open his ears to the instructions which are given there; a little later he learns to manifest his confidence in the sisters who tend him,—for it is in proportion to the care which he receives that the Indian judges of the interest which is felt for him. Our services and our alms convince these poor people that we came here with no other object than to heal their souls and minister to their infirmities; and when we tell them that without the charity of our brethren in Europe we should have no means of succouring them, nor even be able to maintain our own existence, they are greatly affected. The zeal of Christian souls who, in a far distant land, take counsel how they may gain these strangers as brethren in Jesus Christ, touches as much as it astonishes them, and disposes their hearts to examine a religion which inspires so much charity."

The report then alludes to the benefits which the

religious themselves derive from the patient discharge of this holy ministry, and continues as follows: "Here I touch with my finger all the direct woes of our poor human body; and perhaps all the frightful maladies which the hospitals of Europe can display do not suffice to give an idea of what can be engendered by Pagan vice, aggravated by the nature of the climate. As a rule, these unfortunates are covered with sores and vermin, and suffering from diseases of such a nature that even friends and parents wholly abandon them. Let those who dispute the action of Satan in this world cast a glance upon this scene, and they will be forced to confess that the condition of many of these beings admits of no other explanation. Not even madness displays such characters. To labour in such places, and for such patients, is only possible to that charity which seeks to minister to Jesus Christ in their persons." And they are young and delicate women, who have thus left, according to the recommendation of the Gospel, father and mother, the joys of home and all the pleasures of life, in order to waste away in the repulsive duties and stifling atmosphere of an Indian hospital. Let us, for our part, admire the virtues which we do not imitate, and at least contribute, by an easier sacrifice, to maintain the progress of a work which reflects honour upon our holy religion, and in which we see the evidence both of the ravages which sin continues to produce, and of the triumphs of that grace which alone is able to repair them.

We are not surprised to learn from the documents before us that one fruit of the hospital referred to is the multiplication of catechumens. No words can do justice to the difficulties which attend the instruction. The almost incurable mental apathy into which many of these poor creatures have fallen, partly from habits of vice, and partly from constitutional lethargy, opposes a formidable obstacle to their reception of the truths of revelation and the science of the Gospel; but this is only an additional motive for patience and perseverance, and the religious sisters consent to receive as scholars those whom our blessed Lord does not reject as disciples.

In February 1863 the community were gladdened by the return of their Superior, accompanied by seven sisters, emulous to share their toils. It was a timely reinforcement. One had died in the interval, of small pox complicated by fever; and more than one was expending the remains of an energy which had been fatally impaired. The Fathers of the Society of Jesus had formed the wish to establish a new foundation in the southern district of the Mission. On the Feast of the Visitation in this year, a detachment of the religious of Marie Réparatrice removed to Tuticorin, a journey of eight days. The city is inhabited by many castes, all Pagan, with the exception of the Paravas, formerly evangelised by St. Francis Xavier. These, having preserved the faith, earnestly solicited the presence of the religious to instruct their wives and daughters. It was a harvest which they gladly consented to gather in, counting also upon the happy influence which the Christian Paravas, elevated by a higher cultivation, would be sure to exercise upon the surrounding Gentiles. The reception of the European religious in the city was truly cordial. The chief of the caste, escorted by the heads of the city, and the king himself, came to visit them. In a few days more than two hundred children applied for instruction, but for want of space only one hundred and fifty could be received; the rest were dismissed for a time, with unavailing regrets. Soon their occupations multiplied so rapidly that the Superior was obliged to despatch three more religious from Trichinopoly. Not far from Tuticorin, Father Bossan had established two orphanages, both filled by a large number of Pagan children; at his request, the religious of Marie Réparatrice accepted, in 1864, the charge of the girls.

Their labours continued to multiply. At Tuticorin nine widows, who arrived from a considerable distance, presented themselves with a request for aid and counsel in carrying out a work established by Father Verdier, *the Apostolate of Widows in union with the Heart of Jesus.* A little later they were followed by twenty more. They had all been taught to fulfil the duties of catechists, and were accustomed to undertake long journeys in order to baptise a sick child, console a neophyte, or instruct a catechumen. They wished to make a spiritual retreat, and to receive additional instruction in the duties to which they had devoted themselves. By the latest accounts, more than one hundred widows had assembled in this place, lodged in a mere shed, and it had become urgent to erect a suitable building for their accommodation, as well as to provide for their maintenance.

The desire of profiting by the instructions which the religious offered to mothers of families, and which attracted even the sister of the king, led to an unheard-of innovation in the habits of these people. The young unmarried women, hitherto rigorously confined to their own house, accompanied their mothers to the convent, where they were taught to read and write, as well as various kinds of needlework. In a little while the religious found themselves charged with the duty of preparing fifteen hundred women and children for confession.

We do not stay to speak of other places which solicited the presence of these generous women,—of Negapatam, with its 30,000 Christians; or Marava, where the piety of the Indian Catholics reminds us that the

Blessed John de Brito was their apostle; of Madura itself, the capital of the province. Let us hope that each of these cities is destined to welcome them, and that the charity of the Catholics of Europe will supply the material resources, without which their zeal must remain comparatively unfruitful, and the institutions which it is urgent to establish must continue to exist only in the desire of their hearts. Meanwhile, it may contribute to excite the sympathy of English Catholics to know that, while many a city of India would welcome them with gladness, London already possesses, what they demand in vain, a community of the religious of Marie Réparatrice.*

If we have failed to convey to the reader a just idea of the progress and multiplicity of the works undertaken by these religious, of the hopes founded upon them, and of the heavy charges which they involve in their execution, we cannot better supplement our meagre relation than by referring once more, in conclusion, to the testimony of their own acts and words. Impressed with the sense of her responsibility, and the hopelessness of perpetuating even the institutions already established without constant aid from Europe, the Mother Superior of the community at Trichinopoly has again left her sisters to solicit here the coöperation which it would be vain to expect in India. Having sailed from Madras at the beginning of the present year, with the intention of returning in the month of September, she has accepted —in the interests of the Mission, and in order to provide the means of actual subsistence for her own community —the painful duty of urging a personal appeal wherever she may find an ear open to her message. Wanting even the necessaries of life, in a country and amid labours where health can only be maintained by sedu-

* At Harley House, Marylebone Road.

lous care and nourishing food, she asks help for her sisters, who desire to fortify their own strength only to expend it in the service of others. She asks it for widows and orphans, whose lot is cast amid the snares and perils of a Pagan semi-civilisation, and to whom only the charity of European Catholics can secure either the barest necessaries of this life or the promises of the next; she asks it for the sick whom her sisters desire to tend, and the children whom they wish to instruct. It is not possible that she should ask it in vain.

We have seen what the religious of Marie Réparatrice have undertaken, and how far the progress of the faith in India—especially among the women of that land—depends upon their continued labours. If they are not to sink in exhaustion, and be withdrawn from the Mission by the premature sacrifice of their lives, they must be promptly succoured. They are obliged to confess it themselves. "You will be astonished," writes the Superior from Tuticorin to the Superior-General in Paris, "to receive once more a petition for aid. You have made great sacrifices for the Mission of Madura, and many other houses claim your support. It is this consideration which has constrained me to silence, hoping that Providence would relieve our necessities; but I can no longer leave you in ignorance of the sufferings of those of your children whom you have confided to my care. If you can help them in no other way, you will pray for them; and it will be a consolation to my heart to know that yours shares its inquietude. For several months past we have been in want of every thing. We have literally nothing to live upon. One of our sisters told me the other day that her hunger was so intense that she was almost sick; yet it was impossible to obtain bread for her, owing to its cost. For a long time past a person has lent us a few francs at a time, that we might make some purchases in the market; but what afflicts me most is, that we cannot give to our sick the comforts which they need, and which are absolutely necessary to fortify them when they reach convalescence. Poor Mother M. Philippe has just arrived here from Trichinopoly; she was literally dying of exhaustion. She had worked all day, and often during part of the night, to maintain the children of whom she had the charge. The doctor ordered that she should have meat and soup; but you comprehend the embarrassment of the infirmarian. Surprised that Mother M. Philippe did not recover her strength, the doctor—who is a Protestant—asked for an explanation, and we were obliged to confess that we had nothing to give her. He was very much affected, and promised to send her a dinner every day; which, with great charity, he has continued to do. If I beg you, my mother, to come to our aid, it is because I fear for the health of my dear sisters if they remain exposed to such privations.

"But you will ask me, how we can be in such a state of poverty? There are three principal causes of this destitution." She then explains that the price of provisions in that part of India has doubled and tripled; that they have accepted the charge of burdensome institutions, which exhaust all their means, and which they must maintain at any sacrifice to themselves; and that they have had during the year extraordinary charges for travelling, reconstruction of ruinous dwellings, &c. Her letter terminates as follows: "Do not suppose, however, that we are oppressed by this trial. It is a subject of joy to us all to suffer something for our good Master, a proof that our Lord loves us, and a source of hope for the future; for we have learned that there is nothing in this world which deserves to be named unless it bears on it the mark of the Cross."

CHAPTER XIV.

EDUCATION IN INDIA.

It is certain that at an extremely remote date, anterior by many centuries to the Christian era, there were in India schools of great celebrity, in which human science was cultivated with skill and success. Sanscrit was then the language of the learned; the language in which were composed those philosophical, scientific, or literary works, of which some have been recently translated into European tongues, and have excited the astonishment of our Oriental students. The philosophical writings of this period of Indian history, though abounding in false theories, and devoted to the exposition of irrational systems, were evidently the production of men of thoughtful minds and keen intelligence. Their mathematical and astronomical books, though disfigured by theoretical errors, are still more surprising, and contain theorems, axioms, and problems, by the aid of which certain modern *savans* have acquired a spurious reputation, while others have boldly resolved to assign to them a Greek origin. M. Biot endeavours to prove, in his *Etudes sur l'Astronomie Indienne et Chinoise*, "that the Greeks were the parents of Hindoo science;"* an opinion which the researches of Sir George Lewis appear to refute: for though the latter observes, that "the science of Egypt was found by the Greeks to be a nul-

* See *Aristotle*, by George Henry Lewes, ch. ii. p. 38.

lity,"* he is far from attributing to the Ionian or Sicilian philosophers the same superiority over the Indian sages, much less a priority in point of date.

All the works here referred to are written in the Sanscrit language. It was the good fortune of their authors to live under princes who—like Pericles at Athens, and Augustus at Rome—protected the sciences and those who were devoted to them, and thought it no dishonour to employ their own leisure in the study of letters. If the state of India at this epoch was barbarous, it was at least a cultivated barbarism. The Punjaub, the ancient kingdom of Oujein, and afterwards the province of Benares, were the principal centres of Indian science and literature.

The other languages of the country, and especially the Tamul, became in their turn the vehicles of Indian philosophy and literature, and were employed by writers whose names are still greeted with respect by their countrymen. The Persian, or Mahommedan, invasions introduced by degrees a new language—Hindostanee—a compound of Persian and Arabic; on which have been grafted many of the idioms and characteristic forms of true Indian origin. This language also, under the reigns of the Mogul emperors, had its own history and literature. It was during the continuance of this Moslem dynasty—a period for some centuries of almost incessant wars, revolts, and brigandage—that Sanscrit became gradually a dead language, and the sciences ceased to be cultivated. Southern India, owing to its comparative remoteness from the theatre of so many disorders, preserved to a later date its scientific institutions; and at the beginning of the eighteenth century the city of Madura still possessed a flourishing academy. But it was

* *An Historical Survey of the Astronomy of the Ancients,* ch. iv. § 9, p. 288.

in the second half of this century that almost the whole of India entered upon that chaotic phase of its history, during which English, French, Mahrattas, Mysorians, Pindareîs, Gourkas, Seiks, and other races, were to contend together for the remaining fragments of the Mogul empire. In this universal confusion there is little reason for surprise if science, and every institution destined to promote it, disappeared from the land.

The English—triumphing over all their enemies, partly by indomitable courage, but still more by the skilful policy which throughout this contest arrayed one native race against another—had become the masters of India. Their sole thought was to consolidate their empire, and reap the fruits of their conquest. Science, which in other times had given dignity even to Parias, so that they could stand in the presence of kings, had as little interest for the new lords of India as religion. Occupied with other cares, they did no more for literature than for Christianity. As the ancient learning of the Hindoo sages no longer led to honours and distinctions, it was laid aside. Henceforth the highest ambition of the native was to learn sufficient English to obtain employment in a Government office.

There was, however, one institution which survived all these revolutions; preserved by the strange immobility of the Hindoo mind, and which still contributes to maintain the purity of the various languages of India. The village schools outlived the thrones of which the ruins had already been swept away. In every village there exists a school for the children of the neighbourhood; in which a native pedagogue teaches reading, writing, arithmetic, and singing. These schools are so deeply rooted in ancient and national custom, that they are maintained in spite of the golden attractions of Government and Protestant lyceums. But these humble academies do not aspire to be nurseries of science. It became necessary, therefore, after nearly a century of neglect, that the power which had hitherto regarded India only as a new outlet for its commerce, and its inhabitants only as susceptible of taxation, should make some effort to reanimate its intellectual life. The first measures adopted with this view—which imprudently took no account of national customs and prejudices—were as unsuccessful as the temper which inspired them was capricious and unconciliating. It was not till the spirit of proselytism—supple, calculating, and ambitious—gave an impulse to official inertia, which obeyed without ceasing to resent it, that the Bengal Presidency, and subsequently the provinces of Madras and Bombay, were covered with rival schools, maintained in every direction at enormous cost by the funds of the Government or of the various Missionary Societies, whose activity was stimulated by the imperious necessity of keeping pace with, or the deeper gratification of supplanting, one another. It will be useful to inquire, without entering into superfluous detail, what have been the results of Protestant education in India, as they are recorded by capable and impartial witnesses, from whose concurrent testimony there is no appeal.*

The latest Protestant work on India with which we are acquainted is that of Mr. G. O. Trevelyan, published in 1864. It is in the following words that he describes the effect of Protestant tuition on the native mind: "The most ignorant and debased *ryot* (peasant) is a more hopeful subject for the missionary than a young Brahmin, loaded with prizes at a Christian college, who talks like Samuel Johnson and writes like Addison, and will descant by the hour upon the distinction between

* Some of the testimonies here quoted will be found in *Christian Missions*, ch. iii.; the rest are of later date.

Original Grace and Prevenient Grace. . . . . It is not too much to say, that an educated Hindoo almost inevitably becomes a Deist" (pp. 394, 403).

Mr. Lowe, who also speaks from personal observation, thus attests, in his work entitled *Central India*, the same fact: "The native, from the prince down to the household servant—however highly he may have been educated in our British schools—cannot forget his old ways, and, like the dog, returns to his vomit. This is no exaggeration, but a truth painfully witnessed by us every day" (ch. vii. p. 321; 1860).

Captain Herford gives this account of the "rich and fashionable young Bengalese," pupils of English Protestant teachers, in 1862: "These young men had taken in a large amount of European learning, but apparently turned it to no good account. What they had gained from civilisation was only its exterior polish, which they used to gild their Asiatic vices."*

The Hon. Roden Noel observes with great energy, at the same recent date, that "a man like Abd-el-Kader is worth a million of those Hindoo or Moslem gentlemen who have received European instruction, without having imbibed the spirit of Christianity. Our civilisation has but torn from their souls the lingering faith that might have been sheltered under the creed of their race." And then he adds that, by their contact with their Western teachers, "they lost all faith in God, and all regard for man."†

So well are these facts understood in India, that they form a subject of lamentation even to the Pagans. The *Times* of April 27, 1863, contains an account, by its Calcutta correspondent, of the ceremony of conferring academical degrees upon the native graduates in the

* *Stirring Times under Canvas*, ch. xxi. p. 300.

† See Mr. Francis Galton's *Notes of Travel in* 1860, p. 463.

Calcutta University. "The youths so educated," observes the writer, "become Deists. This Deistical state is marked by no little immorality; English vices are fashionable as well as English literature. Their fathers bewail the errors of the rising generation."

"There are instances on record," says the Rev. J. Weitbrecht, a Protestant missionary, "of Hindoo fathers forbidding their sons to visit the Calcutta College, on the ground that *all* the pupils who attain some proficiency *become nasticks, i. e. atheists.*"

Mr. Johnson, Von Orlich, and other Protestant writers, freely admit that the natives consent to accept English education, of which these are the acknowledged fruits, "only in the prospect of obtaining a situation." Yet there are a great number of *Catholic* natives, practical and exemplary Christians, holding responsible offices under the Government; and thousands, the ardour of whose faith has only been increased by the education which they have received in Catholic schools.

A few citations from Anglican and other Protestant ministers will sufficiently confirm the evidence of lay witnesses. They will be found in greater profusion in the work entitled *Christian Missions.*

"The results" of Anglo-Protestant education in India, says the Rev. Mr. Knighton, "have been great intellectual acuteness, and total want of moral principle; *utter infidelity in religion*, combined with an enthusiastic worship of reason and money."

"Missionary schools," says a great Indian authority, in a letter to the *Times*, "do not make more converts to Christianity than Government schools. A most zealous missionary in India assured me, with tears in his eyes, that, after twenty-five years' experience, he looked upon the conversion of the Hindoos as hopeless."

"In almost every part of India," observes the Rev.

Mr. Percival, "the spread of the English language and literature is rapidly altering the phases of the Hindoo mind, giving it a sceptical, infidel cast."

"Results, as they have hitherto manifested themselves," adds the Rev. Mr. Clarkson, "are unfavourable, not only to the Gospel, but to the principles of natural religion." And then he declares that all the missionaries, of all sects, are of one mind in affirming, that though education "undermines the superstitions of the Indians," it has the invariable effect of rendering them "extremely antagonistic to Christianity."

It is not necessary, in such a volume as this, to multiply these testimonies, which seem to be all summed up in the appalling statement of another writer, that the educated native students "have no more faith in Jesus Christ than in their own religion. They believe the Jesus of the English and the Krishna of the Hindoos to be alike impostors."

Yet the Protestant teachers of India have had under their instruction, which they ostentatiously describe to be "purely scriptural," 500,000 children at the same moment, attracted by the material advantages which they are able to dispense; and the sad result of their teaching upon this vast mass of intelligent beings, recorded by themselves, does not appear to have suggested to *one* of them the obvious conclusion, that there is no Christian blessing upon them and their work.

The only consolation with which they soothe their disappointment consists in the reiteration of the singular charge, that the majority of the Anglo-English are no better than the Hindoos. "It is a curious thing," said Dr. Daniel Wilson, lately the highest Anglican official in India, "that one of my chief objects here is to repress infidelity. Our public press abounds with it; our leading men fall into a species of unbelief. Here every thing is called in question openly and arrogantly."* Perhaps, however, the subjects of this accusation may retort that their brethren in England, which is fast approaching the state of Protestant Germany or Switzerland, have lost the right to judge them. "The ravages of infidelity," says a well-known Protestant writer, "are becoming so fearful, and are showing themselves so rampantly in the very penetralia of the Established Church, that there must be a remedy, or the day of Christ's second advent may be declared at hand."† It was apparently this consideration which made the Rev. Godolphin Osborne say to the "Four Archbishops," when they invited the nation to extend the missionary operations of the Anglican Church: "May I not venture to ask, whether the Archbishops are quite sure that a Church, the children of which at home are so bad, is the right sort of church to plant elsewhere?"‡

It need not be said that in India, as in every other land, the Catholic missioners have followed the tradition of their order, the observance of which has made them the most laborious and the most successful educators of many generations of men. To them, and to their predecessors, belongs the glory, which only ingratitude can deny them, of having cultivated every branch of human knowledge with the generous object of communicating it to others, and of affirming by their own practice these two principles: that it should be refused to none desiring to possess it; and that, even as respects the humblest social being, the only limit of intellectual progress is the limit of opportunity.

The missioners in Madura have always been diligent, as far as the meagreness of their resources and the

* Bishop Wilson's *Journal and Letters*, ch. i. p. 7; 1863.
† Howitt, *History of the Supernatural*, vol. i. ch. xi. p. 233.
‡ *The Times*, September 13, 1864.

pressure of still more urgent duties allowed, in the diffusion of education for all classes. Besides the seminary-college of Negapatam, they have established large central schools at Trichinopoly, Madura, Palamcottah, and fifteen other important places. They have done every thing in their power to develop and bring to perfection the village schools. Wishing to profit by the education grants offered by the Government, and by the good will which the exceptional conduct of the Catholic natives during the great insurrection had won from the authorities, they addressed to Sir Charles Wood the following petition:

"*Memorial to the Right Honourable Sir Charles Wood, H.M. Secretary of State for India, from the Rev. Louis Saint Cyr, Catholic Missionary in the District of Madura, Southern India.*

"1. The Mission of Madura extends over the districts of Tinnevelly, Madura, Trichinopoly, and Tanjore, in the Presidency of Madras; from the river Cauvery in the north to Cape Comorin in the south.

"2. It numbers more than 160,000 native Catholic Christians,—viz. about 50,000 in Tinnevelly, 60,000 in Madura, 30,000 in Trichinopoly, and 30,000 in the district of Tanjore. (These numbers are from returns collected by the missionaries themselves.)

"3. The Mission is administered by a Catholic Bishop, Dr. Canoz, who resides chiefly in Trichinopoly, and under him by forty-two Catholic priests, spread over the country.

"4. Trichinopoly is the only station for European soldiers. There is a chaplain there, who receives a monthly salary of 200 rupees. That sum is all that the Mission receives from the Government.

"5. Besides Trichinopoly, there is occasionally a part

of the artillery force at Palamcottah. There are also detachments of native troops at Madura, Tanjore, Negapatam, Ramnad, and Dindigul.

"6. The Mission has a large college at Negapatam, in which about one hundred native scholars are brought up entirely at the expense of the missioners. All the branches of European education are taught. Some of the pupils trained in this college have already obtained Government situations; others have become good schoolmasters; and a few have become Catholic priests.

"7. The missioners have also set on foot five orphanages, in which about three hundred native orphans are brought up. They are trained chiefly in agricultural labour, that they may be able hereafter to support themselves respectably.

"8. There are also two large preparatory schools, one in Trichinopoly, another at Madura, in which about two hundred scholars are educated; and many other smaller schools, attended by a large number of young children.

"9. It is a striking feature of this Mission that the most perfect tranquillity prevailed in all the districts over which it extends during the late Indian Rebellion. This tranquillity must in some degree be ascribed to the large number of Catholics, and to the influence of the Catholic priests.

"10. The Government seems to have acknowledged the great reliance that it can place on the Catholics by sending, two years ago, an officer to the Bishop, and the Superiors of the Mission, with the object of inducing the Catholic priests to persuade their Christians to enlist among the native troops; and it is certain that the Catholic soldiers would never join in any conspiracy against the Government, and would watch carefully over the fidelity of others.

"11. It is consequently the opinion of the memorialist, that it would be good policy on the part of the Government to conciliate the Catholic population, and to give them whatever support it has in its power to grant them.

"12. More especially with regard to the Madura Mission, he proposes to the consideration of Government whether it would not be possible to make the following arrangements,—namely:

"*a.* That the Bishop of the Mission, or his representative at Trichinopoly, should be put on the same footing as the Catholic Bishops of Calcutta, Madras, and Bombay,—*i. e.* should receive a salary of 500 rupees a month. Although there is at present but one European station within the limits of the Mission, it appears that nowhere in the British possessions is there so large a native Christian congregation.

"*b.* That the priests employed in those places that are stations for the native troops,—*i. e.* Madura, Palamcottah, Dindigul, Tanjore, Negapatam, and Ramnad,—should receive a fixed salary of 50 rupees a month; or at least those at Madura, Palamcottah, and Tanjore, which are the capital towns of very large districts. There are some places in the Bombay Presidency where such Government allowances are granted, although native troops alone are there stationed.

"*c.* That the missioners should be entitled to receive, out of the Government grant for educational purposes, a yearly subsidy of about 10,000 rupees, for the support of their colleges, schools, and orphanages. In Ceylon, the

Government gives a yearly grant of 300*l.* to 500*l.* for the support of Catholic schools.

"*d.* The Mission of Madura has many other charges to meet, for the building of churches, school-rooms, and houses for priests, besides travelling expenses from Europe, which weigh heavily on the missioners.

"*e.* During the last twenty years, thirty-five missioners have died in those districts, worn out by excessive labour and privations, in consequence of bad food, unhealthy dwellings, and other like causes.

"In conclusion, the memorialist trusts that the state of this large Mission will be taken into consideration by the Government, and something done towards its support, even if all that is now asked for cannot be at once granted."

The reply to this memorial was kind and courteous, as might be expected from so distinguished a person as the present Secretary of State for India, and contained an acknowledgment of the exceptional conduct of the Catholic natives of India during the insurrection; but no aid was given or promised. Content to spend vast sums annually in support of schools which produce only, by the testimony of their own teachers, atheists and criminals, the Government declined to succour those which alone have been able to form good Christians, and faithful, trustworthy subjects. Imprudent policy! especially at a moment when, as we have learned from Dr. Kay, "the feeling of the natives is increasing very much against this country." "There can be no doubt," observes another witness, "that in Upper India the sentiment of every native who, from intellect, ability, and rank, may be qualified to sit as a representative of his country, is strongly opposed to our domination;"* while Mr. Trevelyan reports, that "at this moment there is a universal belief all over the Punjaub that our rule is to come to an end before this very year (1864) is out." If justice and gratitude did not suggest that the same assistance should be extended to Catholic as to Protestant schools in India, prudence and self-interest might have given the same counsel. Meanwhile, the Christian educators of that land, which England holds provisionally by the tenure of force, can only appeal to their brethren in Europe for the means of maintaining schools which the Government declines to support, though it is not unwilling to profit by them.†

* Arthur Brinckman, *The Rifle in Cashmere*, p. 237; 1862.

† In the height of the Mutiny, 1857, a British staff-officer from Madras arrived in Madura on an *officious* mission. He was charged to ascertain the state of feeling among the large body of native Christians. In an interview with F. St. Cyr and other missioners, he learned, with pleasure and astonishment, that they could not only answer for the fidelity of their Christians, but undertake to place at the disposal of the Government *thirty thousand Christian soldiers*, on condition that chaplains were appointed to attend them in the campaign.

CHAPTER XV.

CHARITABLE INSTITUTIONS OF THE MISSION: ORPHANAGES, AGRICULTURAL SCHOOLS, HOSPITALS, CATECHUMINATES.

In the preceding chapters the divers religious institutions of the Mission have been frequently alluded to; but since 1853 some of them have become so important, both in themselves and in their influence on the Mission in general, that they deserve to have a chapter devoted to their rise and progress.

The alms collected in Europe in 1852-3, when the first little book on this subject appeared, gave the first impulse to these institutions, the want of which had been severely felt before. In truth, it can scarcely be said that the Church is really established in a country before those Catholic charities which are her greatest ornament have taken hold on the habits of the people. As these institutions are a great source of her fruitfulness, so they are a pledge of her vitality and increase.

The Hindoo has always had a great respect and esteem for works of charity; and in the sacred books, "fourteen acts of beneficence" are cited, "which make a person agreeable to the gods and to men." Alms-giving enters into the habitual observances of daily Hindoo life and custom. Unfortunately, the Brahmins had so well practised upon and profited by this national feeling, to their own personal advantage, as to become proverbial for their grasping cupidity. For this reason the Catholic missioners found it necessary to act with the greatest disinterestedness, and to refuse all payment and all presents which were offered to them. They were not unmindful of the words of St. Paul, carried out by the universal practice of the Church in Catholic countries: "They who preach the Gospel should live by the Gospel" (1 Cor. ix. 14); but at the same time they found it more for the glory of God and the good of souls—after the example of the same holy Apostle—to "be a burden to no one." No doubt this course in no small degree has increased the poverty of the missioner; but this is a fault which will correct itself in time: the more the Hindoo appreciates the value of Christianity, the more will he be inclined to contribute to its propagation, and to the support of the clergy who labour for his welfare.

During the first fifteen years of the existence of the new Mission, scarcely any thing had been done towards commencing charitable establishments, on account of the insufficiency of means, which scarcely enabled the priests to live and labour. Since then a good deal has been attempted; several works of active charity have been set on foot, and some with remarkable success. The rise, progress, and rapid fall of many Protestant Mission charities had been most carefully watched, and with no small profit; for *there* could be seen all that could be attempted by purely human means—unlimited resources, great experience, and the highest European skill. The powerful element of excellent Government organisation and official patronage was also at work, in some cases allied to the efforts of Protestant missionaries, in others entirely independent of them. Yet all had failed to realise the good intended, after a short effort at existence, to which novelty and money gave a temporary success. Many of these philanthropic attempts to improve the condition of the native, mentally and physically, sooner or later broke down under the *vis inertiæ* of the native character. This collapse was hastened by the intrinsic unfitness of the instrument employed to succeed in these good works, though undertaken with wise human intentions. As an example of this unfitness, it may be said that the Protestant hospitals, both missionary and Governmental, were unpopular from the first, and totally unused by any save the lowest orders, and this because all caste customs were openly and imprudently ignored in them. The high-caste Hindoo, however poor and suffering, would rather die in sight of one of these hospitals, than accept life and restoration to health, at the expense of social position, by crossing their threshold. In the previous chapter it has been clearly shown how very little the efforts of the Government or of the various missionary bodies in the country have succeeded in advancing the interests either of Christianity or of civilisation by their system of schools and education.

In the year 1853 the first attempt was made by the Jesuit Fathers in the city of Madura itself, by opening a double hospital—one half for the upper, the other for the lower castes. This simple arrangement immediately conciliated the public mind, and numerous sick applied for admission. In this first attempt it was ruled only to admit Pagans; for the funds were too limited to receive any great number of cases, and the Christians were sure of being better cared for by the charity of their friends; whilst the condition of a heathen in sickness is indeed deplorable—destitute at once of all care for either body or soul. In this little Christian hospital they were welcomed with kindness, cared for with much charity, and fed, lodged, and nursed entirely gratis. Many of them, struck with wonder at a spectacle which was so entirely new to them, began more and more to inquire into a religion which prompted such charity; and when the cause of the ceaseless, patient care of their Christian attendants dawned upon them, they asked to be instructed in the faith of Christ and to be baptised. In the mean time, it soon spread through the country, that in the Madura Christian hospital the sick were well cared for and gratuitously tended, and, moreover, that every possible consideration was shown for the caste-customs of the patients. These circumstances attracted attention, excited inquiry, and revived many old existing stories of the ancient Mission. The Jesuit Fathers were again seen carrying out and realising the traditionary charity of their predecessors. This increased their *prestige*, acquired for them much respect and esteem, and was certainly one of the causes of the great increase of conversions which has taken place in late years. For grace acted more powerfully on the minds of those whose prejudices were forced to disappear in the presence of active charity. If good plain buildings could be substituted for the present sheds, and if the funds of the Mission allowed of all those who presented themselves being admitted, an immense good would be realised immediately. With the greatest economy, a sick person can be supported on six or eight shillings a month; and a sum of forty pounds sterling is considered sufficient to make a perpetual foundation for a bed in one of these hospitals. Some of them are under the care of native Christians, superintended by the missioner; others, as has been said more fully in another chapter, are under the care of the European nuns.

There is another class of the destitute poor which has in all times awakened the lively sympathy and maternal solicitude of the Catholic Church. She has always thought it a sacred duty to protect and harbour the poor orphan, who, being without food or shelter, cries out to God for help, and is answered in His name by His holy Church. As soon as ever it was possible to do so, both male and female orphanages were opened, and there was no difficulty in finding poor children—more than enough to fill them.

The Tamul-speaking portion of the Hindoo race is unquestionably the mildest and gentlest of all. Amongst the northern and more warlike portions of Hindostan, female children are often, until checked by British rule, put to death as a useless incumbrance to their parents; but Tamul parents delight in seeing themselves surrounded by a numerous offspring; the ties of family love and affection are also remarkably strong amongst them. Yet, from the constant visitations of cholera and other epidemics, it frequently happens that the parents are carried off, and whole families of children are left entirely destitute.

It is related, that soon after the occupation of Algiers by the French, when the Jesuit Fathers who entered upon that Mission were able to do so, they collected troops of little Arab orphans, whose fathers had been killed in battle or had perished in war, and established agricultural schools. Amongst certain persons, themselves destitute of all practical religion, there exists a strange and unaccountably false logic which, in defence of the assumed "rights of humanity," rises against the will and law of the Creator. They ignore the objective reality of truth revealed by God, and affect to believe that subjective conviction, however erroneous, is sufficient to warrant, and even to sanction, the most grievous and guilty impiety in religious matters. In accordance with this spirit, some of the French officials deemed it advisable, in the interests of philanthropy, to refuse all Government aid to these establishments, unless the children were brought up in the faith of Mahommed, because their fathers had professed it. Christian priests were to be allowed to administer to the corporal wants of the Arab orphans, on condition and provided only that they kept their souls in ignorance of the law of Christ and His holiness. These children were to be duly instructed in the belief and practices of Islamism, and therefore taught, with Mahommedan impiety and readiness, to blaspheme the holy name of Him who died for us—in a word, to prefer Mahommed to Christ.

F. Brumault, superior of the orphanages, appealed against this strange order to Maréchal Bugeaud; and the maréchal decided that the reverend Fathers who had collected and rescued these children were their true parents, and that they had the right to bring them up in their own religion. So holy Church in all ages, convinced of the objective truth of the holy faith it is her mission to preach, has taught its saving truths to the orphan she has rescued from death; for she believes that she is answerable for the souls of men, and teaches that those only shall enjoy the eternal beatific vision who have fulfilled whilst on earth those conditions upon which it is promised to man.

The Church, then, in Madura as elsewhere, true to her tradition of charity, gathered these poor little derelicts to her bosom, and brought them into the fold of Christ. The greater part were Pagans, but they were soon baptised, instructed, and formed to a Christian life. Yet something more was requisite; it was also necessary, besides forming their souls to piety, to provide them with the means of procuring their daily bread. The most intelligent were selected to study, and to advance beyond the mere rudiments of learning imparted to all. A number of the others were sent to two large agricultural farms at Dindigul and Tinnevelly, where those who were likely to have to gain their living by field-labour were duly instructed in agriculture. By proper instruction and regularity of hours they were formed to a life of patient industry; and many who have left those schools have been respectably married, and have become honest fathers of Christian families. The regularity of their early life has made them industrious—industry has placed many of them above want. In these schools all those improvements in European agriculture which are suited to India are duly studied and taught. It is difficult at present to foresee how great the advantages of this system may ultimately be in a social point of view; the good they have already produced amongst the Christian population is not only perceptible, but most consoling and encouraging. There are some of the children who, either from the hereditary intelligence of their caste or from natural aptitude, seem likely to make good mechanics. These boys go to a large establishment at Madura, superintended by a European lay brother, where painting, sculpture, and carpentry are taught, as well as the craft of the white and blacksmith, wheelwright, and tinworker. At Trichinopoly also—a place famous all over Southern India for the quality of its tobacco—there is a manufacture of cigars. During the last year, in all these different establishments there were 617 orphans, well instructed, and brought up to be honest, laborious, and industrious members of society, instead of becoming outcasts and vicious—too often, alas! the lot of the poor orphan.

The orphan girls, too, are collected together and carefully tended by the European nuns, who some years ago devoted themselves to the good of the Christian Church of Madura. In this holy work they are much assisted by the native religious women, who have offered themselves to the service of their neighbour in works of charity. The orphan girls are brought up in habits of industry, cleanliness, and order, and are taught to be good housewives. They are also taught sewing and embroidery, in which some of them excel, although it is not a very useful art in a country where sewed garments are little used. They are likewise taught to read, write, and cipher in their own language—accomplishments entirely unknown to the female sex throughout heathen India. Above all, the greatest care is taken to instruct them all solidly and intelligently in the mysteries of religion, so that they may be able to "render an account of the faith that is in them." Many of these orphans have been well married, whilst others have devoted themselves to God in religious life. None of the native women have been as yet admitted into the order of the European nuns; they form a congregation apart, under the direction and guidance of the zealous sisters of Marie Réparatrice. Many of these well-instructed native women have been carefully taught how to administer the holy Sacrament of Baptism; and hundreds of Pagan children, at the moment of death, are annually by their ministry admitted to the participation of the merits of Christ bestowed by his promise and mercy on those who are "born again of water and of the Holy Ghost."

One more good work of immense value in the Mission remains to be noticed—one of direct and pressing importance, as an abundant cause of conversion and consolidation in the faith. It is the formation and development of catechuminates, where those who, from the conversations of the catechists or exhortations of their friends, are disposed to become Christians receive their instructions. The transformation of a Pagan into a Christian is a labour of love on both sides, both in the teacher and in the person taught. Those who enter the catechuminates must be fed and supported for several days, more or less, according to their intelligence. For long hours each day, seated in circles round an intelligent child, the prayers are learnt by heart by constant repetition. And, as may be seen by the translations given in another chapter, not only the prayers, but the rudiments of Catechism and principal mysteries of faith are thus learnt by heart. During this process, a few times each day the catechists give full, clear, and simple explanations of these prayers and dogmas, the Rev. F. Missioner all the while going about and listening to and superintending all. This constant and persevering care in instructing and forming the neophytes produces the best effect; for very few indeed leave the catechuminates without a good knowledge of their religion, and a very sincere resolution to persevere in its practice. From time to time numbers are baptised together; and those not accustomed to the sight, or of weak faith, would be astonished and almost awe-struck to see the wonderful effects frequently produced by baptism upon the adult. The whole expression of the face is changed, and with it the dispositions of the heart, and the manner and bearing of the individual. In a word, so manifest is the change, that the heathens are struck by it, and the Christians see figured before them those wonderful effects of grace which faith would supernaturally lead them to expect.

These establishments have done immense good, but, like every thing else, require development; they are inadequate even to the present wants of the Mission, and many more would be soon converted if their number as well as size were increased. It should be borne in mind that experience has proved the expediency or almost the necessity of giving daily food to those under instruction; and this is the only human inducement of any sort whatever held out to conversion. The reason of it is, that many are too poor to forego their daily work, and, unless they received the "daily bread" for their bodies, could never spare sufficient time to be fully instructed. By the present system their instruction is fully developed, and they go forth from the catechuminates knowing how to practise and uphold the religion of Christ.

CHAPTER XVI.

MOVEMENT AMONG THE HEATHEN, AND MULTIPLICATION OF CONVERSIONS.

THE earlier Jesuit missioners in Madura, from their first entrance into this sphere of labour until the temporary suppression of the Society, by their incessant toils, their complete abnegation, their apostolic works, and the fervour of their neophytes, had given such an impulse to the propagation of the faith, that the Pagans were being converted literally *en masse.* In the seventeenth century, it was reported that "no missionary converted less than a thousand Pagans annually," while many gained in the same period a far greater number of disciples. Whole villages presented themselves, with their chief at their head, for instruction; and so general was the movement, so regular and sustained, throughout all the southern provinces of India, that eminent Protestant writers have candidly avowed their conviction that the moment of general transformation was at hand, the resistance of Asiatic superstition and idolatry overcome, and the definite triumph of Christianity assured.

But India was destined to share with every other Pagan land the terrible disaster of which the agents, inspired by the spirit of darkness, were already preparing in Europe the future explosion. In planning the so-called Reformation in the sixteenth century, the enemy of man had traced beforehand those formidable incidents of the eighteenth which were its logical and inevitable sequence. "The French Revolution," observes Mr. Carlyle, "is properly the third and final act of Protestantism."*

The suppression of the Jesuits, upon whom, with other religious orders, depended the conversion of the heathen world, was a concession to those principles of Protestantism, which, as far as they related to civil government and social order, had been adopted by the political rulers of almost every European state. The *Encyclopédie*, which was only the scientific expression of the same principles, and which attacked Christianity by the methods which Protestantism had employed in combating the Church, was well described by Victor Hugo in his better days as "that hideous monument, of which the *Moniteur* of our Revolution is the frightful appendix."† Such was the order of those events of evil omen which have exerted so wide an influence upon the destinies of the human race, and of which the Reformation was the first, the *Encyclopédie* and the suppression of the Jesuits the second, the French Revolution the third, and the acknowledged decay of faith in all Protestant lands the fourth.

Nothing is more certain, nothing more capable of demonstration, than that the destruction of Christian Missions in the eighteenth century, and the second burial of the heathen world in the tomb of Paganism from which it was emerging, was a consequence of the Reformation. The proofs of this fact are arrayed with invincible force in the forty-fifth chapter of the work of Balmez, on the contrast between Catholic and Protestant civilisation.

Before the great convulsion of the sixteenth century, Europe was evidently destined, observes Balmez, to civilise the whole world. "How does it happen that

* *Lectures on Heroes*, Lect. VI.

† Victor Hugo, *Mélanges Litteraires.*

she has not realised this destiny? How does it happen that barbarism is still at her gates, and that Islamism still maintains itself in one of the finest climates and countries of Europe? Asia, with all that is a reproach to the human race; . . . . Asia Minor, Palestine, Egypt, and the whole of Africa,—lie before us in a pitiable condition. The sole cause of this phenomenon is *the rupture of Unity*. As long as Unity existed, Christian Europe preserved a transforming power which was able, sooner or later, to make all that it touched European."

The history of twelve centuries, with all its fluctuations, its ebb and flow of good and evil, had furnished abundant proof that a power had been lodged "in the Christian Church," as M. Guizot has observed, "to maintain Christianity," and to transform almost without effort, and in the crisis of their fury, the barbarian nations arrayed against it.

It was only the *Oriental* Christians, separated from Unity, who, as Dean Stanley observes, "abdicated the glory of missionaries;" and even adopted by tens of thousands the new religion which issued from Arabia, and of which the same learned writer remarks, "Mahometanism must be regarded as an eccentric heretical form of *Eastern Christianity*."* Differing from Protestants in the immobility of their errors, the Oriental sectaries resembled them in the bitterness of their disputes and divisions, and in the chastisement which ensued upon them. "Having wearied the patience and long-suffering of God," says the Anglican Dean Prideaux, "in thus turning religion into a firebrand of hell for contention, strife, and violence, He raised up the Saracens to be the instruments of His wrath to punish

* *Lectures on the History of the Eastern Church*, chap. viii. p. 260 (2d edition).

them for it."* For centuries an almost preternatural sterility has afflicted these unhappy Christians, whose decay and ignominy date from the hour in which *they departed from Unity.*

The Orientals, scourged by Moslem despotism, had fallen out of the march of Christian progress and civilisation; but the European nations, deriving force and vitality from their union with the Holy See, had remained heirs of the promises given to the Church, and chosen instruments of that providential mission to all the races of mankind of which Unity was both the source and the object. It was the catastrophe of the sixteenth century which interrupted—though only for a time, since the fertility of the Church was destined to repair its ravages—the work so auspiciously commenced.

"The heart is grieved," says Balmez, "at the sight of the disastrous event which broke this precious Unity, diverted the course of civilisation, and destroyed its fertilising power. It is impossible to observe without distress and indignation, that the appearance of Protestantism was exactly coincident with the critical moment when the nations of Europe, about at length to reap the fruits of long ages of continued labour and unexampled efforts, displayed before the world the fullest manifestation of vigour, energy, and splendour. Vasco de Gama had doubled the Cape of Good Hope, and shown the way to the East Indies. Columbus discovered a new world, and planted the standard of Castille in lands hitherto unknown. Cortez penetrated to the heart of the new continent, and took possession of its capital. Magellan discovered the strait which united the East and West. . . . . The development of mind kept pace with the increase of power. The happy moment had arrived. The fleets of Europe transported apostolic missionaries, whose

* Quoted by Stanley.

hands were to scatter in the new countries the precious seed. But the voice of the apostate, who was to kindle discord in the bosom of fraternal nations, already resounded in the heart of Germany."

From that hour the Pagan principle of national religions was to revive, and henceforth nation was to be so divided against nation, that hardly two of them should be able to combine together, unless it were to injure a third, or to obtain the momentary triumph of some selfish interest, without a thought for the honour of God or the welfare of humanity. In no holy cause or sacred enterprise could they, from that hour, be persuaded to unite. Hostile powers representing hostile religions, watched each other with jealous vigilance, even in the sacred precincts of Mount Sion, and around the tomb of the Saviour of men. Their wranglings were to be a scandal to the impure Turk, to whom their divisions had abandoned the custody of the Holy Places. No longer were Christian fleets to bear to the lands of the heathen the messengers of the Gospel, who were now to be chased on every sea by the ships of England and Holland, and massacred, in the name of religion, by men who had resolved that the heathen should perish in their idolatry, rather than owe the grace of conversion to the ministers of the ancient faith.

Sixty-eight missioners were slaughtered on the same day, and their bodies cast into the sea, between the Island of Madeira and the coast of Brazil, by men who claimed to have revived the primitive religion in its truth, purity, and charity.*

It is true that the hostility of apostate nations was only to yield a new triumph to the Church, more signal than any which she had won since her first struggle with Pagan Rome, and that her Founder chose this very hour

* See *Christian Missions*, vol. ii. ch. ix. p. 147.

to summon to her aid such an army of apostles—the Jesuits alone numbering *twenty-two thousand* at the time of their suppression—as she had never before been able to dispose of in her long warfare against the wiles of the enemy. It was during the sixteenth and seventeenth centuries that she not only recovered millions in Europe who had forsaken her communion, but converted entire nations in the East and West, among whom the Holy Name had been previously unknown. In no country were her apostles more visibly the servants and messengers of the Most High than in India, and in none were the effects of the suppression of the Society of Jesus more disastrous to the Pagan world. That event was followed by the revolutions which convulsed Europe, and for a time closed every nursery of apostolic missioners; so that India was not only deprived of her Christian teachers, but the very source from which alone they could be recruited was dried up. Sixty years were to elapse before the work so fatally interrupted was to be resumed.

But this was not the whole of the calamity which befell India. If the Jesuit Fathers had been banished, the Indo-Portuguese priests remained; and it is not easy to say whether the absence of the former, or the presence of the latter, after the death of those who had been educated and trained by the Jesuits, was the greater evil. Utterly void of the zeal, devotion, and learning of their predecessors, the mercenary agents of a fallen nation which had cast away Catholic traditions, their cupidity and misconduct not only stopped the progress of religion, but made it once more an object of contempt both to Moslem and Hindoo. And contempt, especially in India, is more fatal to religion than the most cruel persecution. If it is a marvel that the Catholic religion, owing to the dignity of its first teachers, and the supernatural force proper to it, had been able to maintain itself in India, in spite of trials almost without parallel, it is not surprising that it had fallen into complete discredit in the eyes of the Pagans, and that conversions had entirely ceased.

When, for the second time, the Jesuits arrived in India, to resume the labours which had been so long suspended, this was the condition of their once flourish- Mission. Their first duty was to restore to religion its purity and majesty, so that even men who hesitated to embrace should be forced to respect it. To this task they applied themselves with the devotion which fears no difficulty and shrinks from no sacrifice. They revived the ancient traditions of the Mission, and restored its ancient customs, adopting for themselves, at the cost of health, and often of life, the austere rule of their predecessors. The difference between them and the Indo-Portuguese clergy was soon felt. Unfortunately these unworthy priests, instead of reforming their own conduct, attacked violently those whose example they were incapable of imitating, and declared open war against them. A new scandal was added to those which already existed.

The different Protestant sects had begun also to arrive in India, and, turning to their profit the neglect of the Portuguese clergy and the decay of religion among their flocks, strove to purchase the momentary adhesion of these unhappy Christians. In some cases they represented to them that their own religion was identical with the Catholic; but the unskilful fraud was soon detected. Meanwhile, India was in a state of confusion and chaos, in which the darkened mind of the heathen could no longer distinguish truth from error. When the Hindoos were invited to become Christians, they would answer with scorn: "Convert yourselves before you attempt to convert us." Retorting upon the Protestant preachers their violent abuse of the Catholic faith, they would sometimes say: "*To which sect would you have me adhere?*" and at others: "Why should we become Christians, when *you tell us* that three-fourths of the Christian world have adopted a creed no way superior to our own?"

But the Church is strong enough, by her union with God, to overcome even such difficulties as these. Her enemies only gave her the occasion of manifesting her superiority, which the Pagans once more learned to recognise. The Protestants, unable to conciliate the aversion of the more enlightened heathen, identified themselves more and more with the basest caste, to whose level they wished to reduce all the others. For a native to profess himself a Protestant came to mean, in the judgment of all castes of Hindoos, that he had resolved to cast off the restraints of decency, and to wallow in an abyss of degradation from which there was no return. At a recent meeting of natives in Calcutta, it was debated whether an easier mode of recovering lost caste than the painful expiation of many years prescribed by the Hindoo ceremonial might not be adopted; but when some suggested that it was possible to join the Christians, it was decided that even an outcast would not improve his position by accepting so infamous a lot. Such is the native estimate of Protestantism and of those who embrace it.

If, however, the Indians had by this time definitively judged both the Protestants and the Indo-Portuguese, in whom they could see no mark of the teachers of a divine law, the instincts of a race naturally disposed to religious contemplation* enabled them quickly to

* "Religion is associated with every act of the people in India."—*Travels in India, China, &c.*, by Mrs. Colonel Muter, vol. ii. chap. ii. p. 38 (1864).

identify the Jesuit Fathers with the earlier apostles, who had won the reverence of their forefathers. In proportion to their contempt for the first was their esteem and admiration for the second. At this day, after the labours of forty years, in which nearly fifty Fathers have found a premature death, the Indians perfectly comprehend that the Catholic is the only true religion of Christ, the only one worthy of their attention. It has regained all its former dignity and influence; and to be a Catholic is now, even in the judgment of the Pagan Hindoos, a title of honour. The neophyte is once more an object of esteem rather than of dislike; and the virtues of the Christians, confessed with a kind of respectful enthusiasm by their heathen neighbours and kinsfolk, form, as in the days of De Brito and Beschi, the most persuasive inducement to conversion. Every new disciple, in the present state of the Mission, becomes himself a preacher to his brethren.

The most experienced Indian missioners, who have themselves borne no mean part in the magnificent revival which has crowned their labours, do not hesitate to affirm, in spite of the severity with which such men judge their own works, that all the ground lost at the time of the suppression has already been recovered. The piety and fervour of the Christians, and the respectful homage of the Pagans, recall the brightest days of their predecessors. The festivals of religion attract multitudes of the heathen, who proclaim aloud that here indeed God is truly worshiped; and men who assert that they would deem themselves defiled if the shadow of a Protestant minister fell upon them, daily stretch forth their hands to touch with reverence the robe of the Catholic apostle, whose life of prayer, penance, and charity excites their honest admiration, and in whose virtues they recognise the tokens of a divine calling.

The present Mission of Madura is only one of *five* distinct vicariates, into which the ancient Mission, as it existed in the time of De Nobili and his successors, has been divided. The *whole* Mission, which in the earlier period numbered 200,000 Christians, contains now more than 350,000. In the part now called the district of Madura, from the city in which the apostolate of De Nobili commenced, the conversions of adult Pagans in the year 1862 were 750 ; in 1863, 1100 ; and in 1864, nearly 1300. That this proportion will henceforth be steadily maintained, or rather, that it will be annually exceeded, the missioners entertain no doubt. If the supply of evangelical workmen, they say, be continued, and the resources of the Mission augment with its wants, "the day is not remote when we may hope to see the whole of Southern India Christian and Catholic." These are the words of a learned and laborious missioner, who has already spent twenty-four years in Madura, during which period he has seen the number of Christians augmented by 50,000.*

A few extracts from the letters of the Madura mis-

* The same consoling facts are reported in the great Mission of Verapoly, containing more than 230,000 Christians. "The Pagans perceive," says F. Marie Ephrem, of the Order of Discalced Carmelites, "that the Catholics are more honest, more moral, more religious, than the sectaries of other religions, and, in consequence, become converts to the faith much more numerously than heretofore. This religious movement," he adds, "is in force in all parts of the Mission of Verapoly;" and so general is its influence, that "the Rajah of Travancore and his first minister, both Pagans, express a sympathy for the Catholic religion which they take no pains to disguise. The latter has recently published a pamphlet, now on my table, in which he speaks as a Catholic would of the august Person of our Lord. He acknowledges Him to be true God and true Man, and he exhorts to the observance of His commandments."

sioners, written in 1864, which throw light upon the nature of their work and its rapid progress, will be read with interest, and form a suitable conclusion to this chapter.

F. Guchen writes thus to F. St. Cyr, who was about to start for Europe on the affairs of the Mission: "You resemble a father of a family going to seek food for his children. This is literally true: we are dying of hunger—if not ourselves just yet, at least our works. In obtaining the means of continuing and extending them, you will be more a missioner than any of us." And then he gives the departing missioner an account of the district of *Ancikarei*, of which he had the charge.

Atticadhe.—A new Mission of fifty-three families, converted during the last fifteen years from nominal Protestantism, and now fervent Christians. "The church is built of earth, and threatens to crumble; the presbytery is a little kitchen, which is also tottering." Formerly notorious for violence, the people of Atticadhe are now devoted to their teachers, and give daily proofs both of zeal and intelligence. "Sir," said one of them lately to a Protestant minister, who was scoffing at his confidence in our Blessed Lady, "when I visited your house, I paid respect to your wife, and that gave you pleasure; do you think I displease our Lord by showing respect for His Mother?"

Another, being engaged in a law-suit, had maliciously assured the minister, that if he gave him his influence with the English magistrate, he might inscribe his name as a disciple. The delighted minister took his cause in hand, and advanced five rupees. When the affair was over, and the Indian refused to keep his bargain, the clergyman, not unreasonably, demanded the return of his money. "What, sir!" replied the other; "the

Jews bought the soul of Judas Iscariot for thirty pieces of silver; I sold mine to you for a whole month, and you think you purchased it too dearly for five rupees."

Veipancadhe.—A new congregation of thirty-one families, formerly Pagan; a miserable church of dried mud, already in ruins; no house; the only ornament in the church a crucifix, falling in pieces.

Callouvilei.—A similar Mission, recently founded, and in want of every thing. "The only decoration of the church is a crucifix, which I lately bought for three rupees."

Amatanacoudhi.—New Mission, composed of 450 Christians, heretofore Pagan. A fair church, but not finished; neither altar nor furniture. "It possesses a crucifix, and a statue of our Lady made by F. Victor Duranquet."

Nedhouncoulam.—Village of twenty-two houses, converted four years ago from Paganism. In 1861 the Bishop desired that a little church should be built for these poor neophytes; but it has still to be begun. "Hitherto they have assembled in a shed, constructed of the wood of their ancient demon-temple; but it has fallen down twice, and now hardly holds together."

Moudélour.—New Mission of twenty-five families; every thing wanted; during the rains one wall of the mud church fell down.

Coulaségarapatram.—A rising Mission, destined to considerable importance. As soon as the inhabitants began to seek Christian instruction, a Protestant missionary caused them to be persecuted by law-suits, which are often ruinous in India even to those who gain their cause. Two of the neophytes were totally ruined; and when the minister sent an agent with an offer to repair their losses if they would profess Protestantism, one of them replied: "Tell your master that we are not base enough to sell our souls for a few rupees. He has succeeded in ruining us—let that content him; to see him speculating on our poverty astonishes us, and seems to us unworthy of a European."

Alankinarou.—More than thirty families have already placed themselves under instruction. "When I consider on the one hand their faith and good dispositions, and on the other the absence of all the conditions favourable to the development of either, Alankinarou seems to me a miracle of the protection of Divine grace." The chief of the village, Pakia-Naden, is a fervent Christian. Only a church and a residence for the priest are required to secure the conversion of the whole neighbourhood. A woman, formerly possessed, said to the missioner after her baptism: "Since you entered my house, the demons have fled from it. What could they do against the Souami?"

Satancoulam.—There are few villages in India in which religion has gained more signal triumphs than in this. After a description of one of his neophytes, whose ardent zeal and piety seem to resemble those of the primitive Christians, and who was occupied in converting all his relations, the missioner adds: "Such are the neophytes of Satancoulam; for I can say, *Ab uno disce omnes.*" One of the latest converts was a young married woman, who has since converted her father, mother, husband, brother, and sister. When she entered the church for the first time, she cried out aloud: "My God, how happy I am! how truly I thank Thee!" "When I baptised her three children, the youngest, only two months old, was unwell. 'I commit him to the care of God,' she said. 'He has now received baptism; and if our Lord desires to take him, His will be done. The child is His rather than mine.'"

We would willingly quote the whole report of F.

Guchen on this remarkable Mission, and its urgent wants. Six demon-temples have already been destroyed by the converted Pagans, who cannot enjoy, for want of means, the consolation of building a church for themselves. One of the most hopeful Missions in India is grievously hindered in its development by the total want of resources, and hundreds of souls are perishing by whom the offer of Christian privileges would be received with joy. F. Tassis, the aged colleague of F. Guchen, adds these words to his letter: "I have read it with tears. What grief to see so many souls perishing because we cannot help them! I have obtained the Bishop's permission to give, as a little relief to their necessities, my own share of bread, wine, and milk; but what are a few rupees to supply the privations of such a multitude?" Will not some generous souls be found in England and Ireland to send help to "*the Mission of Satancoulam*"?

The letters of F. Truical, dated from the city of Madura, are equally interesting and important. In 1855, the Christians under his charge were 600; in 1864, they had increased to more than 2500. During the last eighteen months he had also evangelised seven large hamlets with fruitful zeal. In the largest, a first harvest of 100 souls induced him to build a church capable of accommodating 200. Before it was finished, it was already too small: there are now 400 Christians. In a second populous hamlet a church of the same dimensions was raised, when there were only seven neophytes; "it is now crowded, and will soon be too small." In the other five localities no churches exist, for want of means. "If I could construct at once in them, and in many other places, an oratory in which I could say Mass and obtain a lodging for myself, how rapidly would the conversions spread! how soon would the worship of God supplant that of Satan!"

"Such churches would not cost more," he says, "than from 20*l.* to 25*l.*; yet even so small a sum is not easily procured. I had the greatest difficulty in obtaining from Mgr. Canoz enough to build two this year. The resources of the Mission are insufficient to maintain even the existing institutions, much more to create new ones." Yet a few hundred pounds intrusted to these indefatigable evangelists—who have barely sufficient nourishment to sustain their own strength in so many labours—to relieve the pressing wants of others, build churches and oratories, and pay for the services of qualified catechists, would lead to the conversion of thousands in all directions. How happy shall we be if these pages should contribute to awaken a new interest in so noble a work, and much more if they should provoke a systematic and sustained effort to assure and extend its progress!

From *Palamcottah* the hard-working F. Giuge sends reports of the same success, and the same poverty of human resources. The Pagans, not only in the city, but in all the neighbouring country, begin to confess the holiness of the Christian law; while the nominal Protestants, who are as much Pagans as ever, and are retained for a time by the lavish expenditure of the ministers, only ask for the presence of a priest to cast off a profession which they detest, and a religion which they despise. At *Cameipatti*, three miles north-west of Cayettar, the Father had originally to receive only five or six confessions. "I built there," he tells the Bishop, "a little chapel, and sixty-four new confessions were its immediate fruit. A Protestant church, with its catechist and schoolmaster, have disappeared as if by enchantment."

At *Cailossabouram* there were only a few uninstructed Catholics; a chapel was built, and now "the whole village knows no other temple of God but our humble chapel." At *Pannicoulam* a Protestant minister had fixed his residence, and had erected not only a good church, but a college, in which boys and girls could be separately instructed. "He could not have worked for us more effectively. Of all his flock, only two families remain to him; the thirty-eight others have passed over to us. What did the minister do to manifest his displeasure? He could think of nothing better than to demolish the choir and transepts of his church, explaining at the same time to his followers that he did so because what he had left standing would suffice for the few who adhered to him."

In other places, the very Pagans crowded round the missionary Father to beg that he would bless them and their houses; for while they regard the Protestant clergy as wealthy bankers, from whom they can at any time extract money and protection, by affecting to adopt their religion, they see in the Catholic priests messengers from Heaven, capable of dispensing its benedictions. It is this homage rendered by the heathen to the true religion which, together with the admirable example and joyous faith of the neophytes, makes the future conversion of the country only a question of time. The day of triumph will arrive sooner or later, according to the zeal with which the Catholics of Europe come to the aid of the apostles of India by their alms and prayers. "In six localities of our district," says the same Father, "at least two hundred families only await the signal to throw themselves into our arms. In order to receive this multitude we must have churches, and to build churches we must have money. If F. St. Cyr during his journey in Europe should find any charitable family willing to undertake the foundation of one of our new churches, I request him to communicate to me the names of all its members, that they may be read in the public prayers, and perpetually recall to our Christians the memory of their benefactors. I pledge myself also to institute an annual festival, at which the Christians shall approach the Sacraments, and the missioner shall offer the Holy Sacrifice for the intentions of that family."

CHAPTER XVII.

STATISTICAL ACCOUNT OF THE MISSION.

It is impossible to terminate more appropriately the account given in these pages of the Mission of Madura than by citing the last published report of its Bishop, Mgr. Canoz. That report is dated, Trichinopoly, December 8, 1862.

As the question of *caste* presents itself in connection with almost every department of missionary work in India, the Bishop begins by stating his opinion and mode of action with respect to it. Experience has shown that *caste* is a purely civil distinction, based on social ideas, which exist in the West as well as in the East, but exaggerated in Asiatic communities both by antiquity of custom and immobility of character and institutions. In the Catholic schools and orphanages, the children of various castes play and study together, but will not eat at the same table, nor sleep in the same dormitory. The influence of religion has greatly modified, but has not yet abolished, caste customs. "Doubtless the distinction of castes," observes the Bishop, "is here carried to a ridiculous and often unreasonable extreme; but to aim at destroying it abruptly, to seek to confound all ranks and conditions, and to make an onslaught on that which immemorial usage has consecrated, would be to excite revolution in the country, to injure the interests of religion instead of serving them, and to enter on an idle pursuit of a result which could never be reached. Prudence suggests—reserving altogether its approbation for distinctions legitimate in themselves and indispensable for public order—that we should tolerate what does not contradict the ordinances of the Church, until the progress of time and the development of sound notions shall introduce the reforms which good sense demands." It is thus, we may believe, that the apostolic wisdom of St. Paul would have regulated the question of caste, if he had been called upon to deal with it.

Of the orphanages established at Trichinopoly and elsewhere—which occupy the first place in the Bishop's report—it is not necessary to speak here, as they have been noticed in another chapter. One fact, however, in connection with them, may be repeated in the Bishop's words: "The place of residence of the female orphans in Trichinopoly is attached to a convent of native nuns. . . . . Many of them express a desire to consecrate themselves to God in a religious life. There are six of them in the convent of Trichinopoly at present, who are making their novitiate in a satisfactory manner. I hope their example will bear fruit."

One instance may be added of the feeling entertained towards these institutions by the Pagans. A heathen lady of high caste, banished by her relatives because she had become a widow, had fallen into extreme penury. "Rather than see her only son, ten years of age, whom she loved dearly, suffer and perhaps die, she resolved to send him to the orphanage of Madura, which she knew only by reputation. Madura is forty-five miles distant from the place where the widow dwelt. The poor mother dressed a little rice, folded it in a piece of cloth, and gave it to the child. She placed three halfpence—all she had—in his hand, and, with tears in her eyes, said: 'Go, my child, to the great city of Madura; there you will find a priest of the religion which loves little children;

he will feed you, and save you from dying. Be happy, my son—happier than your mother; and sometimes think of me.'" The boy reached his destination in safety, and has been subsequently baptised. The reader will share the wish expressed by the Bishop, that the child's prayers may obtain the conversion of his widowed mother.

The agricultural orphanages of *Adeikalabouram* and *Dindigul* have been conducted with such excellent fruits—though carried on with insufficient means—as to extort the unwilling applause of men with whom to admire Catholic institutions is always an effort. "The English themselves regard them with a favourable eye, and praise our undertaking. They would encourage them effectually if their official antipathy to Catholics did not prevent them. One of them, a personage of high rank, who had sometimes seen our orphans, said to a missionary: 'This is a grand work; this establishment will produce great results; you could do nothing better for the country.'"

The following extract deserves particular consideration: "We had the satisfaction to see three of our orphans received into the Novitiate of the Brothers of our Lady of the Seven Dolors, as native monks of the Mission. The head of the cultivators at our farm of Dindigul was for some years one of the baptised orphans. Having subsequently married, he has now five children. We have just placed a husband and wife, married from the orphans this very year, as gardeners at the private hospital of the missioners. These examples enable us to estimate what the propagation of Catholicity in India may expect from our orphanages. The good effected is not limited to the establishments, but is diffused abroad. We in this manner rear and form a whole generation of Christians, who will go on multiplying from age to age.

We sow a seed of which the fruit is certain, and will produce a hundredfold. Why have we not means to augment still more the number of our orphans? Alas! cruel necessity compels us to confine it far below our desires." The whole number of orphans, at the date of the last report, was 617. Means of support alone are required to increase it tenfold.

The progress of schools and colleges has been sufficiently noticed in other chapters; but an allusion may be allowed to the "Catechumen Hospitals," of which the Mission counts seven. It is to be wished that, by aid from Europe, their number may be speedily doubled. "They procure the grace of Baptism to a great number of Pagans every year. It is rare to see any one quit them who has not had the happiness of becoming a Christian; *not one ever dies in unbelief.*"

The real object of a Catholic Mission is to establish the reign of Christ in the hearts of men; and though exterior organisation and material means are necessary for the visible existence of the Church, yet unless the Spirit of Christ, by prayer and the Word of God, vivifies her action by speaking to the hearts of her children, her Mission is in vain. By the Divine mercy, the state of the Madura Mission, in a spiritual sense, has of late years made much progress.

The Mission is divided into three districts, each having a separate Superior, who, as the Vicar-General of the Bishop, governs his Mission, and directs all the good works and labours of the Fathers.

The following statistical tables, translated from a tabular sheet drawn up by one of the French Fathers, will give a *résumé* of the material and numbers of the three districts of the Mission, and the whole is brought under view in page 232.

VICARIATE-APOSTOLIC OF MADURA, 1864.

Under the care of the Fathers of the Society of Jesus.

This Vicariate is bounded on the N. by the Vicariate-Apostolic of Pondicherry; on the N.W., by that of Coimbatore; on the W., by those of Verapoly and Quilon, from which it is separated by the southern range of the Ghauts; on the E. and S.E., by about 150 miles of coast, viz. from Nagoor (5 miles north of Negapatam) to Cape Comorin.

THE RIGHT REV. DR. CANOZ, S.J., BISHOP OF TAMAS, VICAR-APOSTOLIC.

COLLEGE OF NEGAPATAM.

Rector—FATHER C. BEDIN.

At Negapatam the Mission has founded and maintains a College, destined: 1st, to form a native Clergy; 2d, to give young Catholic Indians, intended for Government offices, the education they would otherwise be obliged to seek in Protestant schools.

The College consists of:

1. The Scholasticate, or Great Seminary, where five young Religious are studying Theology and the other sacred sciences.
2. The Novitiate; where there are five Novices in course of training.
3. The Little Seminary; where about one hundred boarders are supported mainly at the expense of the Mission.

STAFF OF THE COLLEGE.

European Missioners			6
Native "			2
Scholastics	Europeans	2	
	Natives	4	
	Novices (Native)	5	
		—	11
European Lay Brothers			4
			—
			23
Native Religious of the Congregation of our Lady of Dolors			2

Two Assistant Masters and a Doctor.

The Vicariate-Apostolic of Madura comprises the three distinct Missions of Trichinopoly (Northern Madura); of Madura (Central Madura); and of Palamcottah (Southern Madura); governed by their respective Superiors, under the authority of the Vicar-Apostolic.

Mission of Trichinopoly (Northern Madura).

Comprising part of the Province of Trichinopoly, two-thirds of the kingdom of Tanjore, and all that of Tondiman.

It is divided into two districts: viz. Trichinopoly, with four residences (Trichinopoly, Maleiadipatty, Aöur, Onivor); and Tanjore, with three residences (Tanjore, Pattoucottei, Vallam).

Superior—Father J. Gregoire.

Population.

Catholic:	
Under the jurisdiction of the Vicar-Apostolic	45,000
Under the jurisdiction of Goa	10,000
Heretical (next to none)	
Pagan or Mahommedan	1,141,000
About	1,197,000

Conversions in 1863.

Pagans	228
Heretics	6
	234

Communions	48,943

Staff.

European Missioners	11	
Native Missioners	1	
Scholastics	1	
Lay Brothers	2	
		15
Native Religious of Our Lady of Dolors		14
European Nuns of Marie Réparatrice	9	
Native Nuns	50	
		59
		88

Religious Establishments.

Churches	45
Chapels	174
Schools for Boys	7
Schools for Girls	2

Trichinopoly:

Novitiate for Native Religious.
Convent for European Nuns.
Convents, with Novitiates, for native Nuns 3
Hospital and House of Instruction for Male Catechumens.
Hospital and House of Instruction for Female Catechumens.
Orphanage for Boys.
Orphanage for Girls.

Hospital and House of Instruction at Negapatam.
Hospital and House of Instruction at Tanjore.

Mission of Madura (Central Madura).

Comprising the kingdom of Madura, the province of Dindigul, the kingdom of Ramnad, and of Thevaghinghe (Marava).

It is divided into two districts: viz. Madura, with four residences (Madura, Razakambiram, Dindigul, Pantchompatty); and Marava, with seven residences (Tarougany, Sousseiperpatnam, Ramnad, Poulial, Calladittidel, Souranam, Coutteloor).

Superior—Father L. St. Cyr.

Population.

Catholic:		
Under the jurisdiction of the Vicar-Apostolic		49,500
Under the jurisdiction of Goa		9,500
Heretical (uncertain).		
Pagan or Mahommedan		1,690,000
		1,750,000

Conversions in 1863.

Pagans	543
Heretics	9
	552

Communions	27,800

Staff.

European Missioners	10	
Native Missioners	2	
Lay Brothers	3	
		15
Native Religious		8
		23

Religious Establishments.

Churches	19
Chapels	245
Schools for Boys	4

Boarding-School of Madura.
Farming-School and Orphanage at Dindigul.
Hospital and House of Instruction for Catechumens at Madura.
Hospital and House of Instruction for Catechumens at Sarougany.
Sanitarium for the Fathers on the Ghaut Mountains.

MISSION OF PALAMCOTTAH (SOUTHERN MADURA).

Comprising the Province of Tinnevelly and the Fishery Coast.

It is divided into two districts: viz. Palamcottah, with five residences (Palamcottah, Anakarey, Vadakancoulam, Andipatty, Camunayakerpatty); and Fishery Coast, with six residences (Tuticorin, Puneïkael, Adeikalabouram, Virapandiapatnam, Manapad, Obary).

Superior—FATHER L. VERDIER.

POPULATION.

Catholic:	
Under the jurisdiction of the Vicar-Apostolic	48,000
Under the jurisdiction of Goa	3,000
Heretical	28,000
Pagan or Mahommedan	1,221,000
	1,300,000

CONVERSIONS IN 1863.

Pagans	337
Heretics	28
	365

COMMUNIONS	38,683

STAFF.

European Missioners	11	
Native Missioners	4	
Lay Brothers	1	
		16
Native Religious		3
European Nuns of Marie Réparatrice	12	
Native Nuns	17	
		29
		48

RELIGIOUS ESTABLISHMENTS.

Churches	99
Chapels	50

Convents, both for European and Native Nuns, at Tuticorin.

Schools and Workshops for Young Women, at Tuticorin.

Convents, both for European and Native Nuns; Farming-School, and Orphanages for Boys and Girls; Hospital and House of Instruction for Catechumens, at Adeikalabouram.

Convent for Native Nuns at Vadakancoulam.

Schools for Boys	2
Schools for Girls	1

Summary.

Population.

Catholic:		
Under the jurisdiction of the Vicar-Apostolic	142,500	
Under the jurisdiction of Goa	22,500	
		165,000
Heretical		30,000
Pagan or Mahommedan		4,052,000
		4,247,000
Churches		163
Chapels		469

Conversions in 1863.

Pagans	1,008
Heretics	43
	1,051
Communions	115,446
Baptism of Heathen Infants in danger of Death	5,000

Staff.

The Right Rev. Vicar-Apostolic.	
European Missionaries	38
Natives	9
Scholastics (nine of whom are Native)	12
Lay Brothers	10
	70
Native Religious of Our Lady of Dolors	25
European Nuns of Marie Réparatrice	21
Native Nuns	67

CONCLUSION.

If in this volume we have spoken of *one* only of the Indian Missions, we do not forget, nor do we wish the reader to forget, that the same apostolic works are in progress in many other parts of the peninsula. The Fathers of the Society of Jesus, who are labouring in Madura, in the Presidency of Madras, are also devoting themselves to the same holy work in the provinces of Bengal and Bombay. The excellent priests of the Congregation of Foreign Missions, the centre of whose operations is in Pondicherry, claim also our respectful gratitude and admiration.

The Right Rev. Dr. Fennelly, at present the senior Vicar-Apostolic in India, is labouring at Madras with an Irish clergy; and the same nation has furnished some priests to Agra and Hydrabad. Other Catholic missioners are scattered over the various parts of the vast continent of India; but in no part, except perhaps the Vicariate of Pondicherry (which formed a portion of the old Mission of Madura), is there the same rapid progress of Catholicity at present.

But it is of Madura only that we proposed to speak in these pages, and of the progress of Christianity in a sphere celebrated in the annals of the Church by the almost unexampled success of its earlier apostles, and for ever associated in the hearts of Christians with the great and venerable names of De Nobili and De Brito. In no part of India has the same amount of apostolic labour and life been expended.

We have seen how the edifice which *they* built up was sustained through half a century of storm and trial, so that the floods raged against it in vain; and how its fair proportions have been increased, and its ancient beauty revived, by a later generation of evangelical workmen. There is, perhaps, no page in our missionary annals—crowded as they are with memorials of Divine grace and power—which reveals more plainly the hand of God than the twofold history of the Madura Mission. It enters now upon a third epoch; and they who have had no share in its earlier glories are invited to coöperate, according to the measure of their gifts and opportunities, in gathering in the final harvest which they did not sow, but which it will hardly be possible to reap and garner without their assistance.

The wants of the Mission are urgent and pressing. They have lately been enumerated by F. St. Cyr, and are chiefly these:

1. Debts incurred recently, owing to the multiplication of indispensable institutions, the constant increase of conversions, the construction of churches and chapels, and the rapid augmentation of the price of provisions. To discharge these debts is the first condition of continued success. They compromise the future of this immense Mission, especially in a country where the legal interest of money is twelve per cent.

2. The maintenance of the *personnel* of the Mission, including 70 priests and lay brothers.

3. The support of 21 European and 67 Indian nuns, and of 25 native religious men.

4. The payment of native catechists, whose services are indispensable; of schoolmasters, to whose number large additions should be made; the entire maintenance, including food and clothing, of 200 students of the Seminary College, and of the preparatory schools, as

well as of 50 orphans of Christian parents, for whom no aid has been received from any quarter.

5. The little hospitals, which exert so powerful an influence for good, and the establishments for catechumens, which are the source of so many conversions, must be maintained, and, if possible, increased.

6. In more than twenty new Missions, recently organised, it is necessary to build small churches, or at least chapels, to assemble the neophytes together, and to form centres of attraction for the heathen.

Dindigul, the chief locality in a Christian district of 5000 souls, has for its principal church the dining-room of an old English dwelling-house. A church should be erected here which may do honour to our holy religion; it will be dedicated to St. Joseph. The royal city of *Tanjore* has also no suitable church; that which it is proposed to construct will be dedicated to the Precious Blood of our Lord. *Ramnad* and *Pamjampatty*, centres of Christian populations of 4000 and 5000 souls, have for churches only miserable sheds. Other central churches,—such as *Souranam*, with its 8300 Christians; *Couttelour*, with 4300; *Sousseipperpatnam*, with 6200; and *Pattoucottei*, with 5000,—remain unfinished, for want of the necessary funds.

Moreover, many of the missioners, who die at the rate of two every year, and who must die in such a climate when deprived of all the comforts of life, have no other abodes than wretched huts, dark and damp, and infested by snakes and other dangerous reptiles.

To these various charges must be added the serious cost of travelling; the distribution of alms among a vast population of poor Christians; pecuniary aid to those who suffer from unjust legal prosecutions, instigated by hostility to the Catholic faith; the annual repairs and maintenance of churches, presbyteries, schools,

&c. &c.; as well as the many incidental expenses which, in so vast a Mission, it is impossible to avoid, and, without European succour, impossible to meet.

The sole contribution upon which the Madura Mission can count, in support of so many and great undertakings, is derived from the annual grant made by the Society of the Propagation of the Faith. The sum allotted by the Society, upon whose assistance all the Catholic Missions throughout the world depend, has never until the present year exceeded 2000*l.*—about enough to build *one* modest church in England or France!

The English Government, which gives readily vast sums in support of the Anglican Establishment and of Protestant education in India, pays a moderate salary to a single chaplain at Trichinopoly, who has charge of the British Catholic soldiers. This is the sole donation offered by England to the Catholic Missions in India, though they maintain institutions full of promise for the welfare of the country, and number more than 1,000,000 native Christians. "The English magistrates and officers," observes F. St. Cyr, "often express their astonishment that we, with means so insignificant, have been able to do such great things, while their ministers, with their immense resources, have done comparatively so little; but this barren testimony adds nothing to the joys or hopes of the missioner, except the consolation of having deserved it. He must continue to look elsewhere for more substantial support."

It has been observed more than once in these pages, and to this thought alone they owe their publication, that the Indian Mission can count upon no other benefactors than the Catholics of Europe. In their hands, under God, its future destiny reposes. Not only will it be impossible to undertake the new works which the numerous conversions have made necessary, but even those already existing can hardly be maintained without prompt and effectual aid. If we marvel that God should have suffered the extension of His kingdom to be dependent upon human agents, and that so close a relation should exist between the progress of a purely spiritual work and the fluctuating supply of mere material accessories, we may perhaps find an explanation of the mystery in this consideration, that no other plea would have left space for the action of lay Catholics, nor have permitted the faithful to coöperate in a work so dear to the Church, and so acceptable to her founder, as the conversion of the Gentile world. They can never be indifferent to so magnificent a privilege.

We only repeat the testimony of the most experienced Indian missioners when we affirm once more, that the triumph of Christianity in Madura, as in the other provinces, depends now upon the adequate application of human means. The zeal of the Apostle is the first, but not the only, condition of success. Conversions will be, in some measure, proportioned to the abundance of the subordinate helps which he may receive. It is possible to look only on what has been called the romantic side of Christian Missions, and to be fascinated by the unearthly elements of wisdom, heroism, and charity which make up so large a part of their history; but they have their practical aspect also; and as the first missioners of the Church, while gazing upon the cloud which hid their ascended Lord from their view, were admonished by angels not to lose time in that wistful contemplation, but to set themselves to the long and painful task of which, after manifold toils, a death like their Master's was to be the issue, so it will be our wisdom to pass at once from sterile sympathy and admiration to the most fruitful labour of willing sacrifice and generous coöperation.

Nor is it a *new* work, of which the future might be a matter of doubt or speculation, which solicits European aid. That work has already a history of three centuries. The evangelists are in the field, and their disciples also: the first able and willing to emulate their predecessors; the second still cleaving to the faith which neither sorrow, nor neglect, nor abandonment, nor corruption, have been able to quench. If, then, there be any charm in the memory of the Indian apostles long since gathered to their rest, any persuasiveness in the voice of those who have succeeded to their office; if it be worthy of Christian zeal and love to perpetuate the work of Xavier and De Nobile and De Brito, and to cultivate the vine which *they* planted; if it be expedient to succour the weary labourers who are fainting under the sun of India, and to give them, not the luxuries which they despise, but the bare necessaries without which they can neither work nor live; if young and delicate women, who have gone forth from France or England to minister to Indian wives and daughters, are not to waste away under intolerable privations; if the cry of hundreds of widows, and the prayer of thousands of children, have power to awaken Christian compassion; lastly, if the consolidation of a multitude of existing churches, and the building of an equal number of new ones, the care of 200,000 Christians who have already accepted the faith, and the conversion of vast masses who are only waiting to know and embrace it,—if these be worthy objects of sympathy, and bear with them a message sufficiently urgent and imperious to reach our hearts, the Mission of Madura will not have appealed to us in vain, nor be left without the succour which it asks from those who alone have power to give it.

POSTSCRIPT.

IN the last page of this book a tribute of thanks must be registered to some of the Europeans in Southern India, whose kindness can never be forgotten. And first to the humblest class, who, by constant self-denial, have continued during a long course of years to bestow their generous alms.

The hard-earned pay of the poor Catholic soldier has raised many a handsome monument of charity in India, and supported many a priest, to whom the Government he served had refused the smallest help. In many places in the Indian peninsula large churches have been built, ground purchased, and a missioner established, by the united efforts of Catholic soldiers. The unseen and all-guiding providence of God has sent forth the Catholic soldier, apparently on a mission of death, but really on a mission of life to thousands. The grace of God has supported and strengthened faith in his heart, and inspired him to raise the Cross in benediction over himself, as a sign to the heathen around him. Whilst loyalty has strengthened his arm, and guided his courage in the day of battle to stand by his colours till death, so faith has strengthened his hope, and guided his soul in its combat for heaven; and his death-bed has been blessed and hallowed by the numerous charities of his life. He has forefelt the assurance of the value of alms-deeds; and how good it is to have laid up "treasures in heaven, where the moth consumeth not, and thieves do not break through and steal."

Could we now behold them in the possession of those crowns which they have gained by their generous self-denial on earth, and their sacrifice of many comforts for the love of God; could we hear their song of triumphant joy,—we should be struck at the greatness of their reward. Could we hear with our outward ears the advice their happy souls would give us, how loudly and exultingly would they cry to us, "Go thou and do the like!"

Also a word of thanks is due to some amongst the civil and military officers, who have shown much kindness and given help in time of need; but to none more sincerely are the thanks and gratitude of the missioner of Madura due than to the English medical officers, who have always given their gratuitous services with a readiness and generosity truly admirable. For weeks at a time have their services been rendered with unfailing, generous patience; and more than once has the English doctor in the district lodged and nursed at his own expense the Catholic priest in cases of severe illness, and, by his skill and charity, restored him to life and usefulness.

THE END.